Driftless Spirits

Driftless Spirits

Ghosts of Southwest Wisconsin

Dennis Boyer

PRAIRIE OAK PRESS
Madison, Wisconsin

First edition, third printing, 2000

Prairie Oak Press
821 Prospect Place
Madison, Wisconsin 53703

Typeset by Quick Quality Press, Madison, Wisconsin
Printed in the United States of America
by Sheridan Books, Chelsea, Michigan
Illustrations by Owen Coyle

Library of Congress Cataloging-in-Publication Data

Boyer, Dennis.
    Driftless spirits: ghosts of southwest Wisconsin / Dennis Boyer.—1st ed.
    p.   cm.
    ISBN 1–879483–35–1 (alk. paper)
    1. Tales—Wisconsin. 2. Legends—Wisconsin. 3. Ghosts—Wisconsin. I. Title.
GR110.W5B69 1996
398.2'09775—dc20
                                                                96–43649
                                                                CIP

For Sam and Ben

Contents

Part Eight   Dane County

Part Nine   Green County

Introduction

Like many people, I have written far more books in my imagination than in reality. But as far-reaching as my interests might be, the idea of writing about ghosts never occurred to me until a few years ago.

It was not as if I thought ghost stories were unworthy of my efforts. I always rated the *Legend of Sleepy Hollow* as one of North America's premier stories.

Rather it was more a matter of my belief that I lacked the temperament for such writing. Most of my adult life had been spent on coldly methodical pursuits which left little room for consideration of life's mysteries.

A move to an old farmstead in Iowa County, Wisconsin, changed all that. Rehabilitation of century-old buildings and stewardship over hollows, woods, creeks, and springs forged a new seasonal rhythm in my life.

A rash of unexplained events prompted some questions of my neighbors and consultation with my back-to-the-land advisers. They opened my mind to an incredibly rich tradition of spirits in the land. A little collection entitled *Ghosts of Iowa County* resulted from those conversations.

After that I was off and running. Calls, postcards, and impromptu visitors brought more ghost stories to my attention. Suddenly I was the local ghost expert.

This new-found role came as a complete surprise to me. The surprises were just beginning. Soon came leads to folktales and more ghost stories. But so did strange calls about UFOs, crop circles, and United Nations mutilation of cattle.

Within a few years I had amassed files on odd stories spanning southwest Wisconsin and beyond. The decision to limit this collection to southwest Wisconsin stemmed from a strong sense of place embodied in those stories and the recurrence of some themes different from those of other areas.

My efforts met with a fair amount of curiosity and a number of questions: do you believe in ghosts?, do the people who tell these stories believe them?, and how do you pick which stories to use?

The question of my own beliefs finds no simple answer. It is not easy to collect such tales without a difficult combination of independent judgement and openness. Suffice it to say that my personal experience includes incidents not easily explained by science.

My sources exhibited a wide range of involvement and belief in their tales. Some were quite serious. A number of these were almost obsessed. Some combined elements of belief and whimsy. A few were totally tongue-in-cheek.

The stories found in this collection are representative of dozens, if not hundreds, more which can be found in southwestern Wisconsin. The selection process is based partly on my personal preferences and partly on how the sources and I hit it off.

High value was placed on off-beat tales which were imbued with local flavor. I was looking for more than the stereotypical haunted house stories. If a story presented a strong sense of place, a sense of history, and revealed something about the source, well, that was exactly what I was looking for.

Many stories in this collection have been restructured to fit the chronology of events within them (not the meandering of often interrupted conversations). In other instances some liberties were taken in order to fill gaps in the stories. Finally, it must be conceded that here and there my clarifications may tread perilously close to embellishment.

I hope that the stories retain their fidelity and the flavor representative of the experiences and insights kindly shared with me. If not, my apologies to those who feel that I may have strayed from their intent.

Readers will note that sources are not identified and that locations are often left vague. In part these omissions flow from the sources' embarrassment at the prospect of public exposure as tellers of ghost tales. But for many, privacy concerns are even more compelling. It is amazing how much unwanted traffic will come down your driveway after your property is identified as a haunted site.

Ethnic terms and tribal references are entirely within the context of the sources' remarks. No insults are intended.

Often the leads and background that establish a story context are as important as the sources' tales. My appreciation for these goes out to Robert White, Louren Gutherz, Doc Goodweiler Dan McKinley, John Bergum, Elsie Dudek, Rocky Ryan, Joe White Eagle, Dutch Hershberger, and the Eco-Spirituality Group at Sinsinawa Mound.

The interest and encouragement of many people sustained me through the years. Thanks to Jo Stoll, Susan Lampert Smith, Walt Bresette, Paul Gilk, Elmer Manatowa, Neil Giffy, Melva Phillips, John Hess, Terry McDonald, Bill Klosterman, Donald Wanatee, Helen Loschnigg-Fox, Owen Coyle, Dave Gjestson, Dean Connors, and patient editor and publisher Jerry Minnich.

Most of us recognize the debts we owe to those who have passed on. It would be odd to pay homage to the living in a collection of spirit tales without also pausing for warm remembrances of those no longer with us. To Jonathan Weikert Boyer, Dorothy (Hudak) Weikert, Tom Saunders, John Lawton, Billy Kuehn, John Beaudin, Noah Hege, Mom and Dad Bresette, Hilary Waukau, Victoria Gokee, and George Vukelich: Thanks for the memories.

Finally thanks to my family: helpful and loving spouse Donna Weikert and our sons Samuel Paul and Benjamin Erwin and my daughter Lori Garrett. May we have many more opportunities to share stories.

Dennis Boyer
Iowa County, Wisconsin
Summer Solstice, 1996
(the night too short
for most ghosts)

PART ONE

Iowa County

Winny Beaujeau
The Frenchman's Ghost

THE TALE OF the Frenchman's Ghost pops up here and there along the lower Wisconsin River. It might be thought of as a relic of voyageur days if not for its connection to an unusual bit of Iowa County lore.

In the area between Highland and Avoca there is a folktale about the Morrey Creek Medicine Woman. The story concerns a woman of mixed European-American and American Indian background. The details suggest tribal connections within the Algonkian groups, possibly Sac. She is often linked to a character called the Frenchman's Ghost.

A chance bit of research on old Chippewa legends enabled me to see the connection between the pioneer tale and its ancient American Indian roots.

The pioneer tale involved a French Canadian trapper's ghost. The trapper's name was Winny Beaujeau. He was a trickster while alive and was even more so in his ghostly form.

Those of us who tracked the local variations on the Winny Beaujeau tales were in for a surprise when we learned of the long and pervasive presence of *Wenebojo* within Chippewa folklore. As it turned out, many of the Woodland North American tribes had this supernatural practical joker as a character within their creation stories.

The *Wenebojo* of the Great Lakes area is a strange half-god and half-mortal who possesses the power to assume animal shapes and recover from mortal wounds.

But this *Wenebojo* is mainly a character of deception and deceit. He is hardly a role model. Indeed, many stories about this trickster hold him up as a negative example.

The Winny Beaujeau of the Morrey Creek stories is a slightly different character. The deception quotient remains high even though it is all in good fun. This ghost, however, lacks any godlike attributes. He is thoroughly human.

Listen to the echoes of a ghost story with prehistoric roots.

One Avoca family knows the Winny Beaujeau story well. The blood of the Morrey Creek Medicine Woman flows in their veins.

A young man of this family, John, has taken it upon himself to preserve the family's stories. He guards the old photo albums and memorizes the names and places of past generations.

"We usually heard him called 'the Frenchman's Ghost,'" said John. "Mom's grandparents talked about him all the time. They were quite old. For a long time I thought the ghost was somebody they had known.

"It was the old people who called him 'Winnie Beaujeau'. For the young people he was the 'Frenchman' or 'Frenchie' or even 'the Frog'. But my Dad would laughingly call him 'Whiney Bozo.' We heard that this ghost haunted Morrey Creek and across the Wisconsin River and up the Pine River. But I've learned he often changed his appearance. He was a scary giant on Coumbe Island. And an old one-eyed man on Long Island."

John knew nothing of *Wenebojo* and old Algonkian myths. For him it was simply an old family Halloween story.

"At first I thought of it only as a story. I mean, I never saw a ghost. But Grandpop told me toward the end of this life that he did see the Frenchman's Ghost.

"I wish I had asked him more questions. He only mentioned that a deer he shot turned into the Frenchman and got up and ran away. And he also talked about a giant catfish that he fought for an hour trying to land and what comes up with the line in his mouth but the Frenchman with catfish whiskers on his face."

🌾 🌾 🌾

In the far northwest corner of the town of Pulaski, tight against the Iowa-Grant line, there is another version of the story.

"Oh, that Winny Beaujeau," laughed Ed, the retired farmer. "He's the ghost thief. Yeah, whenever we got something missing around here it's a good bet that our sticky-fingered Frenchman's got it. He hauls the loot to an underwater cave near the mouth of the Pine River. He has a big treasure there.

"He was especially fond of the booze. For years people around here have known that. Oldtimers knew not to leave the whiskey jug sitting out. Heck, even a barrel of hard cider wasn't safe.

"You laugh. I had a case of beer taken right off our porch.

"That wasn't my only run-in with the Frenchman's Ghost. No, he made off with a brand new Stihl chainsaw.

"Yeah, I got up to tap a kidney one night. It must have been around one o'clock. Anyway, I heard a noise out in the garage. I thought it might be a raccoon. So I went out in my jockey shorts. Grabbed the old baseball bat off the porch just in case.

"But when I threw open the garage door I saw a tall black figure. All decked out in black. Even black over his head.

"He let out one hair-raising scream and ran right over me. Yeah, no kidding. I had a boot print on my chest.

"Well I screamed too. First 'cause I was scared. Then because I saw that rotten son of a ghost hauling down the lane with my chainsaw."

🔥 🔥 🔥

A feedmill truck driver from Arena treasures his deep Wisconsin River valley roots.

"Dad's family helped settle old Helena," Steve mumbled while wiping his brow. "We have relatives scattered from Sauk City to Wauzeka. With big gangs at Arena, Lone Rock, and Avoca.

"It was from an old aunt at Avoca that I heard of a Frenchman's Ghost by the name of Winny Beaujeau. And it was from her that I learned that Winny Beaujeau was the granddaddy of all local ghosts.

"Not only does he play tricks on the river by Avoca and Gotham, he pops up in almost every ghost story from the Dells to Hazel Green.

"He's involved with a bunch of hell-raising ghosts at old Helena. He's connected to, if not the Ridgeway Ghost himself. He passes through Mineral Point to haunt the old inns there.

"He may be the basis for ghost sightings like the ones at Eagle Cave. Or the one at the Sinsinawa Mound. Even perhaps the ghost fisherman down in Lafayette County. But I've come to know him in one special form. I've seen him ever since I was a boy. Always's at night. When camping on the sandbars. When fishing the sloughs. Or just by those boat-landing bonfires where plenty of stories are told.

"He's an old man I've seen ever since I was twelve. The winter I turned twelve I helped an Avoca cousin check traps on Saturday and Sunday morning. My part of the trapline was on Avoca and Goodweiler

Lakes. I often heard an old man laughing and coughing up snot when I made those early rounds before sunrise. Then one cold night I saw him in the light of a full moon. The old bugger was emptying my traps ahead of me. He laughed and laughed.

"Boy was I mad. I yelled at him and cursed like no one ever heard a twelve-year-old curse. Then I made a big mistake.

"I decided to chase him. This was on Avoca Lake. Instead of running all the way around—it was plenty mushy along much of the bank—I thought I'd cross the ice. Problem was the ice was only a few nights old.

"I got about halfway across the narrowest spot on the lake, then I crashed through. I struggled in the cold water, but I just couldn't pull myself up on the ice. Finally I got tired and numb. I think I passed out.

"But it felt like someone grabbed the collar of my coat. I can't remember much except that I woke up coughing water with the old man's face right above mine. I blinked my eyes a few times and he gave me a big grin. When I sat up he shuffled off in a hurry, laughing into the early dawn.

"I saw him many times after that and he always gave me a blink of a strange looking eye."

🌿 🌿 🌿

A restored farmhouse near Clyde is the retreat and sanctuary for a retired teacher. Born to the area and familiar with the hills and creeks, Ralph finds himself back home after an absence of over thirty years.

"Winny Beaujeau?", he laughed.

"Oh, that old tale of the Frenchman's Ghost! It just goes to show how people can get a story messed up. Look what they do with the Bible and the Constitution!

"You say it comes from old Indian creation stories? That doesn't surprise me. All things come from Creation. There's really nothing outside of Creation so the whole of authentic human experience must draw on this source.

"Do I sound obtuse? Sorry, I tend to get philosophical—maybe even spiritual—about such things.

"What is a ghost, anyway? We immediately think of spirits of the dead. But that's only part of the riddle. All living things—and I include the idea of ecosystems and a living Earth itself—possess a spirit. This spirit or ghost is the undying essence of these things.

"I believe there is a unity of spirits into one spirit. Under this view any ghost that we might experience in one particular place is really part of a larger pool.

"Place! That's the key. The spirit in all things comes out in ways unique to time and place. So that a ghost like Ridgeway's is invoked by us but evoked by the broader spirit.

"By place I don't mean just individual sites like a house. I mean entire regions. Regions capable of generating their own 'feel'. That's why you're finding these things in Iowa County. We have an abundance of that Southwest Wisconsin spirit essence. It's probably been here since the last ice age. Maybe longer.

"We're not alone in this. I've traveled the world. Place is always the key. I've felt it in the Black Hills and in the Black Forest. I've heard it in voices from Hopi country to the Scottish highlands. Don't tell me it can't be found at Red Cliff and the Apostle Islands.

"So what do these ghosts of place do for us? Well, if we opened our ears and hearts we would find that they are road signs toward a path of balance. They warn us, cajole us.

"Ghosts are outside of science. But that doesn't mean that they are province of the ignorant. Ghosts are the core of all folklore and myth and the basis of much transcendent experience.

"Science—or I should say the elevation of science to a religion—kills off ghosts. That is why we live in such a fragile time. We are on the brink of a mass extinction of our ghosts. If we lose our ghosts we will lose our basic connection to our past, to each other, and to the Creation itself. Such a world will be devoid of joy and magic.

"I've been criticized for these views. Some of my hyper-ventilated fundamentalist neighbors think I'm attacking the church.

"I'm not against religion per se. I'm a lifelong Lutheran. But I'm against dead technocratic churches devoid of mystery.

"Remember the third leg of the Trinity! It's the Holy Ghost!

"Well, this has been a long-winded introduction to Winny Beaujeau. But you should know you're seeing the tail end of the ghost stories. Because of that you have a tough job ahead of you. Almost like painting a picture of a buffalo and then telling people that there were once sixty million buffalo.

"You missed a big crop of oldtimers around here that died in the Sixties and Seventies. People with old country grandparents who heard their first ghost stories in other languages. They had many variations on Winny. Some you could barely recognize, but you always found the connection in the tricks.

"For the old Germans there was Wilhelm Baugau. He was the ghost of a Prussian army deserter. With the old Norwegians it was Willy Bolle. He was the ghost of a mutineer off a whaling ship. With the Swiss was something about an old mountaineer that yodeled from the rocky bluffs. With the Bohemians it was a goat herder. With the Cornish and Welsh it was a miner.

"Some would even say that Winny was *The Voice* at the Battle of Wisconsin Heights that scared the soldiers. So there you may have your Indian connection.

"But always the tricks. The usual stuff. The meats stolen from smokehouses. The potatoes pilfered from root cellars. And you hear an inordinate amount of hunting, fishing, and boating variations. Game spooked or driven away. Lines cut or stringers robbed. Mooring lines cut or canoes weighted down and sunk.

"Now a certain amount of this you could discount or write off as bad luck. After all, these are robust activities where accidents are commonplace. But it's that common feature of the old man that gives them credibility and plausibility.

"My own encounters all fall in this category. There's the archetypal old man that I ran into as a kid and keep meeting to this day. He's a little different each time. Dressed differently. Even talks differently. But there's enough similarity there to let you know that it's the same character.

"Now I've always seen him at boatlandings or sandbars. Always at dusk or later. Usually comes marching up spouting insults and cracking jokes. Whatever you're doing—tying a knot or splitting some wood—he can find something to say about how stupid you are.

"Now others have seen him away from the river. I've heard some who say he'll come in a tavern for a drink.

"How do I know that he's a ghost and not some wise-ass senile citizen? Well I've had him disappear on me instantly more than once. And when I tried to follow him into sandbar willows one time I found he didn't leave a track where I sank to my ankles.

"But he knows I'm catching on to him. Last time we met he winked at me and said, 'You're learning, boy'.

"So if you're off on this great ghost hunt, let me give you some advice. First, what you don't know can hurt you. So be open to everything. Take in everything.

"Don't just collect ghost stories. Analyze them. Understand them. Connect them. Revisit them periodically from new perspectives. Keep up these efforts and you'll learn many strange things. When you get to know the ghosts of a place you will know the place and its people in a way you can't presently imagine."

Mineral Point's Haunted Hotels

EVERY VILLAGE AND city in southwest Wisconsin has a ghost story or two. Most follow the usual haunted house pattern of objects moving on their own or fleeting sightings in hallways.

But for sheer numbers and odd circumstances Mineral Point outstrips them all.

A few of the stories stem from old miners' stories and the Black Hawk War. However, the vast majority are linked to the buildings and sites that once served as inns, hotels, stage coach stops, and boarding houses.

It seems that in Mineral Point commercial lodging establishments always figured in stories involving the macabre or untimely deaths. Apparently there was a time when superstitious travelers avoided overnight stays in Mineral Point in favor of Belmont or Dodgeville. This dark undercurrent was one of the reasons Mineral Point lost its bids to remain a seat of government.

Today the sightings are more benign. Indeed they probably act to attract more visitors than they repel. One finds an almost proprietary attitude toward the ghosts. The accounts also betray disappointment at the lack of dependable regularity of sightings.

There are spirited arguments that arise out of these proprietary attitudes. And the irregularity of sightings tends to blur distinctions between individual ghosts. It is impossible to settle all those arguments or clarify all the confusion between sightings. Therefore this account will deal with the main themes found in Mineral Point ghost lore.

Perhaps the most unique among the lodging ghosts is the so-called "Triple-Decker Outhouse Ghost." Outhouse ghosts appear in a number of rural stories. What is unusual here was the presence of multi-story outhouses attached to the exterior of hillside boarding houses.

Mere mention of the Triple-Decker Outhouse Ghost brings forth a multitude of questions about multi-story outhouses. The structure calls forth an image that is either laughable or revolting depending on the earthiness of the listener.

The questions inevitably turn to the mechanics of the structure before the nature of the ghost. The delicate inquiry generally centers on "where does the hole go?" and "do people sit one above the other?" But the simple answer, that the chutes offset to the side, dispels laughter and concern.

A few multi-story outhouses still exist, although none have been used in years. The haunting continues in the form of board rattling and moaning.

"The ghost comes from a boarder who crashed through rotten boards and was killed on the stone ledge at the bottom of the pit," claimed Erwin, local shopkeeper.

The most common wandering spirit in Mineral Point is the "Salesman's Ghost" which is associated with a variety of lodging sites.

"He sold patent medicines and is the cause of a lot of after-dark knocking at doors," claimed Minerva, the bank teller.

Although not seen much recently, the "Stable Boy Ghost" is a tale that goes back to territorial days. It is a multi-site ghost associated with the lower end of High Street and with the Prairie Springs Hotel just south of the county line on Highway 23.

"The apparition is of a lad of about twelve, wandering about, with a horse collar and driving harness over his shoulder," wheezed Harold, the farm implement mechanic.

Clergy are often the butt of folklore humor. Mineral Point's "Pastor's Ghost" is in that vein. This ghost apparently stems from a circuit-riding preacher of the early days. He is generally thought to be a Methodist and appears to be loosely patterned on a clergyman who frequented the early inns of the mining settlement.

"He was a man of a large appetite and was known to claim the choice portions if others were slow to heed the call to the dinner table," smiled Walter, the deacon.

"He is still seen wandering and sniffing the smells of eating establishments. He also is known to cast disapproving glances into tavern windows."

Skullduggery of various sorts also figures in several ghost stories. A few large rocks supposedly hide the foundation of a pioneer inn on Henry Street. An early lodging on Vine Street is alleged to have a hidden cellar chamber. On South Street a long-gone boarding house once had a secret passage to a mine tunnel.

All three locations were alleged sites for hidden bodies of murder victims of local power plays. On the Henry Street site it was a rival to the leaders of the early territorial government. On Vine Street it was a land speculator. On South Street it was one of the organizers of the original railroad charter swindles.

It is said that these three ghosts do not walk abroad. Moans from their crypts are their only protests of violent fates.

A stalking ghost on Ridge Street is referred to as the "Bounty Hunter." He walks the area along Highway 151 between Commerce Street and Fair Street.

"He was an Englishman sent to retrieve a Cornish fugitive," confided Norman, the bed and breakfast owner. "There was a widow with a big house here on Ridge Street. She rented rooms. In one such room the Englishman died before he caught his prisoner."

Then there are the more fleeting references to ghosts of travelers who never made it out of Mineral Point alive. A tinware peddler who still rattles pots. A medicine show charlatan. A gypsy patriarch.

There are also a few stories hard to pin down.

One boarding house apparently saw double duty as a brothel, in which an overweight customer died of exertions of the flesh. His ghostly manifestation still roams Mineral Point robbing wash lines of ladies lingerie.

A more informal "lodging" in the form of a shed near the brewery served as shelter for hoboes off the railroad. Apparently several were found dead over the years. The theories range from exposure to harsh Wisconsin winters to a serial killer.

Their ghosts are said to play harmonicas and boil mulligan stew along the creek near Liberty Street.

Virtually all the above ghosts tie into the Walker House along old Water Street. Walker House also has its own extensively documented ghost. The on-premises spirit is alternately referred to as the "Walker House Ghost," the "Hanging Ghost," or "Caffee's Ghost."

All the names refer to the ghost of one William Caffee who was hanged for the inexplicable murder of a friend in 1842.

The hanging took place across the way from the Walker House. The inn itself was the center of the carnival atmosphere that ensued from the presence of nearly five thousand spectators.

Grandfathers in Mineral Point still entertain children with tales of Caffee's insolence. The tales of Caffee's defiance and anger span his incarceration, trial, execution, and afterlife.

It is said that Caffee showed no remorse. He baited witnesses and his jailers. He yelled insults to passersby. It is said that on the eve of his execution he made a grisly request for his last meal: a raw slice of trial Judge Jackson's liver. The following day he beat out a funeral march on the lid of the coffin in the wagon carrying him to the gallows.

Perhaps it is Caffee's personality and the context of other Mineral Point ghosts that explain the spirit encounters in and around the Walker House.

"Oh my, yes, the Hanging Ghost," clucked Esther, a former Walker House kitchen worker. "Sometimes I think that old Caffee took it upon himself to battle all the other wandering spirits we have in this town. Half of what goes on in the Walker House is ghost fighting and fussing.

"By that I mean the door slamming, door swinging, and doorknob rattling. And the doors locking and unlocking themselves and the locks spitting out keys.

"In the kitchen it was banging pots. Oh my, yes, they rattled on opposite sides of the room. Sometimes in all four corners.

"The ladies had the hardest time. The younger and prettier they were, the worse it was. Yanked ponytails, snapped elastic, and indecent tickles.

"Then when Caffee was visible he took different forms. Might be a boy or an old man. Or a mutilated corpse or a floating cloud.

"Some people had the idea that Caffee was most active when there was a crowd about. This being his reaction to the mob at his hanging.

"This fits with the old story told by the railroad watchman. He said he sat down for a rest and fell asleep and had a dream. I know for a fact he was nipping at the bottle and passed out. And he was too scared for it to be a dream or alcohol fantasy.

"He claimed he saw the hanging scene. He was there! Oh my, yes, right in the crowd. Caffee was on the scaffold. Drunken miners cheered. Militia drums beat out a death march. Boys chased dogs through the streets. Preachers offered loud prayers. Peddlers hawked their goods. There was even a chanting Indian medicine man.

"The watchman then saw Caffee's body drop with a loud snap. In an instant every face in the crowd had turned into Caffee's face.

"Caffee was a tricky guy and he's still a tricky ghost."

Wisconsin River Cliff Ghost

THIS IS A "two-for-the-price-of-one" ghost. There are two versions about a female spirit who dwells just downstream from the Lone Rock bridge on the south shore of the Wisconsin River.

One version centers around a young Winnebago Indian woman who loses her true love to the murderous acts of drunken soldiers. It is said that she set out to wander in mourning and found her way to the cliff above the river.

The site was considered a holy spot and was often used for prayer and vision quests. The young woman fasted and prayed day after day and night after night.

After a week with no insights or signs the young woman resolved to cease her mourning at sunset. She sat patiently through a strangely silent day—no birds, no splashes of fish or turtles, and no wind in the trees. The last bit of the sun's orange ball sank in the west when she rose to walk away.

Suddenly she heard a young man calling her name. She looked down at the water and saw her true love swimming. He beckoned her to join him in the river. In her joy she dove into the river and disappeared under the surface.

It was said that a tricky river spirit had lured her to his world. After that her spirit was destined to stay at her last place on earth.

The other version revolves around a young settler woman during frontier times. The basic storyline is the same: broken heart, grieving, and longing for lost love. The irony here is that in this version it is Indians who have killed the young white woman's groom-to-be. The settler woman version also contains the twist that the young woman throws herself into the river to avoid capture. One might venture to suggest that how the story is told reveals a lot about the teller's position on race relations and the displacement of Indian people.

The oldtimers say that the River Cliff Ghost caused lots of trouble in the riverboat days. Just like the Lorelei of the German Rhine River stories, she would lure boatmen into foolish acts. Boatmen would hear singing at dusk and, while diverted, would end up stuck on the always changing sandbars.

More recent accounts have the River Cliff Ghost crying and wandering the stretch of Highway 133 west of the bridge. It is also said that odd whimpering sounds can be heard by canoeists when the wind rushes through the hemlocks that grow out of the crevices in the cliff.

It is a lovely spot on the Wisconsin River. Late in the day you can face Long Island to the north and easily imagine Indian bark craft and settler flatboats plying the waterway.

On a quiet day (which seldom occurs on the heavily visited river anymore) you might hear and see flocks rise out of Bakken Pond on the north side of the river. Some say that if you pick the right day—a day at a time of year when the sun will set directly over the river—you will see a "green flash" at the moment of the setting and that in that flash you will see a young woman walking on the water's surface.

The Pecatonica Fisherman

IOWA COUNTY CANNOT claim this spirit fellow solely as its own. It must share him with surrounding areas.

The Pecatonica Fisherman is one of the few genuinely regional ghosts. Tales of this ghost pop up in Grant and LaFayette counties and Northwest Illinois as well.

"He favors the Pecatonica branch that flows from Mifflin southeasterly to Darlington," says Russell, an old-timer from Rewey. "He has been seen on the Pecatonica east branch near Blanchardville, on the Yellowstone, on the Galena and even on the Platte."

One must wonder about these claims of widespread sightings. Are they part of the fisherman's tradition of stories that grow with each re-telling?

But our Rewey source believes that Iowa County's claims are the only ones with a long tradition—back to the Great Depression some say. "The Pecatonica Fisherman is seen mostly in the early morning mists in spring and summer. Quite often he is seen just off the road near bridges between Mifflin and the county line."

By all accounts he is an older gentleman with wire-rim spectacles and a neatly trimmed white beard.

Take your pick on the origins of the Pecatonica Fisherman. Some say he was a judge, some a medical doctor, and some a pastor. All conclude that he is where his heart always was: roaming the streams of southwest Wisconsin.

There are varied (and sometimes contradictory) observations about the old fellow:

"Sometimes he is seen with a stringer full of fish—even holding them up for display!"

"I heard he had a sad look during the late 1980's drought—the fish sure weren't biting then."

"My brother saw him fishing in a dried-up crick, with the line laying in the dust."

"I first saw him with a fly rod, but years later I saw him with a cane pole."

It is said that the fish in this area are more active jumpers than elsewhere, repeatedly jumping completely out of the water. This activity occurs in spurts that can last an hour or more, during which no bait can tempt the fish to bite. It is said that the old gentleman is catching them and letting them go as a way of teasing fisherman.

Few have been able to get close to the Pecatonica Fisherman. If you approach him he drifts away on the morning mist.

A young fellow from Belmont has a strange tale to tell.

"My granddad told me about the ghost, but I wrote it off as an old story. Then when I was down by the stream—I won't say exactly where—a scary thing happened. I was looking straight down into a deep pool and noticed that my reflection seemed very bright, almost sparkly. BANG! All of a sudden a second reflection was beside my own. An old man in a fishing outfit. I jumped and whipped around. No one was there. I looked at the water again. The reflection was still there. I looked over my shoulder again. Again no one. I closed my eyes. A hand touched my shoulder! I was so startled that I slipped and fell in the water."

In taverns down that way the gray-beards sometimes hoist a beer and toast "to the man who's permanently put up the 'gone fishing' sign."

The Bethlehem Road Ghosts

GHOST STORIES HELP us develop a sense of place. And when those stories spring from different eras in the same place they provide us snapshots in time.

Bethlehem Road is where my family lives. The road dead-ends at our farm. Our move to that location was not just a change in location but also a change in time.

While we find it to be a special spot, there is little to distinguish it from similar fingers that branch off of Military Ridge.

The area contains the headwaters of Lee and Martin creeks and is bounded by Berg Road on the east, Sinbad Road on the west, Mount Hope road on the north, and Highway 18 on the south.

When we moved there we were not aware of any ghost lore. Two old bachelor farmers preceded us at that location. They were reclusive and few people in the vicinity ventured onto the dead end road.

Bethlehem Road's main traffic consisted of funeral processions to Bethlehem Lutheran Cemetery once or twice a year and the annual Memorial Day observance at the same burial ground.

The auction and farm equipment sale at the Lee brothers' farm brought hundreds of vehicles back this little used road. It was immediately after the sale that the strange signs began.

Friends were helping us clean up sale remnants on a mild spring afternoon. Suddenly the wind quickened. A dusty whirlwind formed in the barnyard and followed the road away from the farm. Minutes later another whirlwind went through on the same path. Then another.

We did not keep a precise tally of the whirlwinds, dust devils, and associated smaller swirling eddies that often accompanied the bigger whirlwinds, but they continued through that spring and summer. We witnessed dozens of them and assumed that plenty of others occurred when we were not looking.

A Chippewa Indian spiritual teacher came that spring to help us celebrate our move. We asked him about the whirlwinds.

"This is a special place with many, many spirits, and some know that it is time to leave this place to its new occupants," said the medicine man.

He visited often that summer—sometimes alone on vision quests and sometimes to guide a pupil on a fast. It was clear that the medicine man was drawn to the woods and prairies on the north end of our farm. He asked permission to bring a group to our farm for a weekend.

More than fifty people assembled there in late August. They built a main lodge and a sweat lodge. Elders from Canada told the traditional stories and conducted sweat lodge ceremonies and pipe ceremonies.

On the second evening of the gathering a sudden storm came up and blew down tents and split and toppled trees. Lightening struck repeatedly. Luckily no one was hurt.

A group was conducting a sweat lodge ceremony at the time. Some came out saying that the lodge was totally still. Others said that spirits swirled within the lodge.

The next year the spiritual gathering was repeated at the same site. This time more than a hundred people attended, including traditional healers and teachers from Central America and Southeast Asia. Again the second evening was disrupted by a sudden and violent storm. The group was assembled in the great lodge they had built. The rain pelted the lodge and the wind lashed at it. The elders attempted to continue on with their teachings but the storm intensified. In an instant the wind picked up in a roar and tugged at the lodge itself. The people were directed to grab onto the nearest lodge pole and hang on.

The wind gave a massive final burst that jerked the lodge several feet up in the air, along with many of the people who were hanging on. A few seconds of terror were quickly followed by an eerie calm.

The elders sought the answer to this occurrence in the sweat lodge the following day. When they emerged they spoke of a storm spirit or "wind rider" who had joined them in the lodge.

"It is a Winnebago woman from long ago," said one.

"She died here, cold, hungry, and alone," said another.

There were disagreements about the proper course to be followed. Some wanted to leave, others wanted to conduct a ceremony for the storm spirit. In the end the only consensus reached was that a food offering to the spirit would be placed in the woods.

That group never returned to our farm after that.

We later had occasion to make friends with some Sac and Fox people from Iowa. When they heard the story they asked if they could visit the site. We said yes and for a year or two several at a time would stay in the woods for a few days at a time.

In recent years neighbors would sometimes ask, "Are the Indians staying in your woods again? We heard drumming last night."

But when we would check with our Sac and Fox friends in Iowa they told us no one had been on our farm in a long time.

We do not see the whirlwinds anymore. But lightning continues to strike frequently in the vicinity of the lodge.

Little is known about what went on in the Bethlehem Road area between the removal of the Indians (1830s) and the homesteading era (1860s to 1900).

The area is on the edge of the old lead mining district, so squatters and mining prospectors are the likely first white inhabitants.

East of the house is a straight row of massive white oaks. A local forester pegs them as one hundred-fifty to one hundred-seventy year old trees. So someone was "landscaping" at a fairly early stage.

Shortly after we moved in, our walking exploration tours brought us to an old stone foundation about a half-mile north of the barn. We almost missed it, as it is hidden in a grove of large red cedars on the brink of the ridge.

The stonework is pretty much intact, although there is no sign of the wooden structure which rested on it. It looks like the building had a half-cellar with an outside stone stairway access.

Later explorations turned up foundation remnants of a variety of outbuildings. A spring still flows about a hundred feet from the main foundation.

A friendly neighbor filled us in on the history of the old site. "The last of the old-time pioneers lived there—a man named Tommy Lee," said Lester.

The stories about Tommy Lee that later came to our attention were colorful and tinged with scandal. Everything from illegitimate birth into a local family to bodies hidden after drunken fights.

Our neighbor seems to have the more credible version.

"Tommy Lee was an old man when I was a kid. He farmed a little—kept a cow or two and some chickens—mostly he hunted, fished, and trapped. He ran a line of fishing set-lines all the way down the Harkin and Otter to the Wisconsin River. In the winter he trapped raccoon, muskrat, and mink.

"He was quite an outdoorsman. The outside of the house was covered with drying hides and the air was always filled with the smell of smoking meat or fish.

"The old boy kept a team of horses. But mostly he walked through woods or kept to the crick bottoms. He was seldom seen. Luckily for him, since he operated outside the law. Old Tommy didn't have any use for conservation wardens or fish-and-game laws.

"In the 1930s he finally bought an old Model T. He didn't have a real road back to his place. It was more of a logging trail. But he bounced his Model T across the ruts to bring milk to the cheese factory at the junction of Berg Road and Highway 18.

"Then during World War II sometime—I was gone in the South Pacific—he took ill. He wouldn't leave his homestead. But eventually he got so weak that they just took him to the Norwegian Nursing home in Stoughton.

"He died shortly thereafter. His house was torn down and a farmer built some sheds with it. You can still smell the fat from the animal hides on the lumber."

I did not give the story about Tommy Lee much thought until we started to host a group of hunting friends on our farm in deer season. Around the kitchen table after the opening day hunt, four friends worked on hot soup and brandy. One by one they recounted the day's events. The last one, a city friend, added an afterthought to his hunting story.

"By the way, I ran into an old guy down by that back creek—Martin Creek—all alone. I almost bumped into him. He was wearing a blue wool coat and black cap and leaning up against a tree. Couldn't see him in that valley shadow. Not a bit of blaze orange on him. The old geezer was toting a real antique—a rolling block carbine with an octagonal barrel. He looked to be at least eighty years old. Introduced myself and he just said, 'Call me Tommy'. I didn't have the heart to run off the old guy like you said to do with trespassers. Do you know him?".

At the time the thought of Tommy Lee crossed my mind. Another round of brandy washed it away.

A few months later a pickup pulled into the barnyard. A bearded young fellow rolled down the window. "You didn't happen to see any coon dogs wandering around?", he asked. "Me and my buddies were hunting near here last night. The dogs were running a coon. Then it sounded like they had one treed. We hustled down there and the dogs were running in a gully. I shined the light and we saw an old guy chasing the dogs with a whip. He looked up at us and yelled, 'Get out of my woods!'. It's odd because we're sure we were on my buddy's dad's farm."

The dogs never did turn up.

The next deer season another hunter told me of an old man in a blue coat standing in the woods.

Shortly thereafter a neighbor asked me if someone was trapping in my creek bottom. "Somebody walked through the valley carrying a load of traps," he said. "Whoever it was had his hands full. He was hunched over under the load and walked like an old man. Kinda shuffling. I yelled at him but he didn't stop. I was up on the hill and didn't want to walk down and back up, so I let him go."

Each deer season after that produced a report of an old man in a blue coat.

I asked my Chippewa friends about these reports. They told me that someone must shoot a deer and leave it at the site of Tommy Lee's house.

🌾 🌾 🌾

In the spring of 1995 my son Sam and I sought refreshment at Tommy Lee's old spring on the north slope facing Martin Creek.

A rough hill farm covered with woods and brush brings plenty of opportunity for discovery even after six years of occupancy. So there was no sense of surprise in spotting a previously unnoticed stone pile to the east of the spring.

The pile drew my attention as a convenient collection of likely building stones. Block-like and angular, the stones showed some evidence of hammer dressing in the old mason's style.

Closer inspection and careful movement through the gooseberries and prickly ash offered the possibility that the pile was not a random stack of building stones. No, the pile was clearly rectangular with ninety degree corners still evident at the base.

A tumbled down outbuilding? A collapsed root cellar? No matter, the stones would serve well in an outdoor fireplace or flower bed retaining wall.

At the time, the main question was how I might best get the stones out of the heavy brush and up the hill.

As this question was pondered we circled the pile and probed under some outlying flat flagstones. A bright white rock was kicked loose.

The pile and surrounding stones were typical Iowa County moss-covered beige and grey sedimentary rock. But the white rock was clearly not native. No, it was a fist-sized marble chip with polished surfaces.

A gravestone!

Those who know Southwest Wisconsin well know of its many old private farm cemeteries. So a gravestone in the woods is not exactly a rare find. But between hunters and local historical societies most such burial grounds have been located and cataloged. Thus new "finds" are unusual. The steep slope also was out of character.

Thoughts of stone building projects were soon replaced by many questions. Who was buried here? When was the site used? Why the odd location? What was the purpose of the stone structure?

No one in the neighborhood had any answers. Everyone suggested that the secrets were buried with Tommy Lee. It looked like a very cold trail to follow.

A total fluke produced a lead. My folktale research took me to New Glarus to discuss Swiss lore. It turned out my source there had a grandfather who shared a room with Tommy Lee during the old hunter's last year in a nursing home.

"My Grandfather—on Dad's side—loved to talk about Tommy Lee", said Edwin with a slap to the knee.

"He really thought old Tommy was quite a character. All the hunting and fishing stories and hints at moonshining and poaching.

"Now you must understand that we Swiss always got a good chuckle out of a Norwegian story. Especially about those rock-farming Norskies over in Iowa County.

"It was sort of like the way white people use to view those minstrel shows in blackface. There are plenty of Swiss where you just say the work 'Norwegian' and they split a gut. You don't even have to reach the punchline.

"But Grandfather and old Tommy had plenty good give and take on this joke stuff. Old Tommy could dish it out pretty good about stingy Swiss, too-smart-for-their-own-good Swiss, and dour and depressed Swiss.

"Grandfather said old Tommy was not consistent about his stories and that in Tommy's last six months he didn't always remember who or where he was. And old Tommy was given to fits of anger and panic.

"But yes, there was mention of burials over by the old cabin. But such a tangle of tales I've never heard.

"Grandfather said that old Tommy first talked of having buried his 'sweetheart' down on that hillside. The nursing home people told Grandfather that there was no record of Tommy having a family.

"So there was one mystery.

"Then Tommy told him about his 'lost darlings.' Like little ones lost to disease like was common in those days. 'Little darlings under the rocks', I think was another phrase he used.

"Doesn't make sense, does it?

"Well if you think that's goofy, hold on to your hat. Old Tommy would also get to raving about a 'well of spirits.' Some kind of a hole that ghosts lived in. Ghosts that bothered him all night long.

"But old Tommy also would boast that he shut the ghosts up. By that I mean he trapped them in the hole. Something about piling stones over the entrance of a cave.

"That's not all. Old Tommy would also talk about people falling down his well and that his root cellar fell in on someone. Then to top off all this mish-mash there is what happened after Tommy died. Some lawman—state or county I don't know—came to question Grandfather.

"Apparently those Wisconsin River disappearances were going on even back then. I guess there was some suspicion of a serial killer.

"Grandfather simply told of old Tommy's incoherent rantings. I don't think it led to any solution, but it sure made Grandfather wonder whether it meant that Ed Gein-type things went on out at that cabin.

"An old friend of mine from the Highland Masons told me lots of ghosts were seen near Tommy's old cabin. And there was something about crying coming from under a pile of rocks.

"Sounds like you have so many ghosts over that way that you can't sort them out.

"I don't know if Tommy Lee killed anyone or buried anyone. I don't know if spirits were chasing him or if he was just crazy. And I don't know if the place is haunted. But I can tell you old Tommy was haunted. Haunted 'til the day he died."

The Bethlehem Lutheran Cemetery was the site of the pioneer church in the area.

A carved and polished piece of granite at the burial ground notes that the church was organized by a number of Norwegian immigrants with the help of North America's first Norwegian Lutheran pastor.

A careful inspection of the well-maintained grounds reveals the remnants of the church foundation in the center of the acre plot.

No one is surprised to hear of ghost stories associated with a graveyard. But we lived close to this one for more than three years without hearing a murmur of a ghost tale.

In the early summer of 1991, overnight guests reported hearing a voice in the graveyard. They attributed the gruff but feminine voice to lovers' quarrels that occur in parked cars in secluded spots.

A few weeks later, other visitors heard crying from the direction of the graveyard. The crying rose and fell on a pattern of soft whimpers and heavy sobs.

In mid-July a friend brought a load of draft horses.

"Sorry I'm late," apologized our friend. "I had a flat tire in Iowa and then the spare barely got me to the next town. By the way, I saw the strangest thing as I turned into your lane. A woman was kneeling in the middle of the cemetery, swaying back and forth. Funny, she looked like she was wearing an old nightgown. Maybe one of those white dresses from India. Wonder if she has a child, husband, or parent buried up there?"

I thought it odd, too. Especially when I remembered that there are no graves in the middle of the graveyard. The church once stood there.

In early August a conversation with neighbors tuned to talk of the old Bethlehem Lutheran Church. The eldest present offered up a chronology of the church history. But the other neighbors disputed some of the facts.

"I remember that being in 1939, not 1935."

"Didn't the railroad passenger service stop about then?"

"Someone said the church burned down, but I don't remember the fire."

But somehow they smoothed over their disagreements and blended their various versions into a consensus about "what really happened."

The eldest participant took charge of the discussion again to recount anecdotes about church life in the old days.

We all laughed at a tale of a pastor sliding down the hillside after an ice storm and looking quite comic with the seat of his pants torn open.

Another tale recounted the consequences of a runaway team, wagon, and bouncing coffin. The coffin was recovered in a nearby pasture and the team and wagon showed up in Edmund the next day.

"But the saddest thing I remember is how that woman from the county home would run away and hide in the church," said the older neighbor.

"I don't remember if she was mentally ill or retarded—we said 'crazy' or 'a little slow' back then.

"Life wasn't so great there in the 'poor farm' days. We often wondered if someone was abusing her. I don't remember any other runaways.

"She didn't go straight to the church. But in a few hours she would show up there. Usually she was found kneeling in front of the pews, swaying back and forth, crying and praying. Some of the big Bible thumpers said she was speaking in tongues.

"You know, I think she died shortly after the church was gone."

After that I thought a lot about the possibility of yet another ghost in the neighborhood.

Every couple nights I would take an evening walk past the old churchyard. Never heard or saw a thing on these walks.

It was a mild fall evening—late October or early November—when the next incident brought the story back to mind.

I was about to go to bed when I noticed I had left a light on in the barn. When I went outside I immediately thought I heard an infant crying. Maybe an animal sound. But I thought I should investigate.

I walked down the lane but the sound seemed to retreat.

When I turned the corner at the graveyard I saw a blur in the middle of the cemetery. A woman in a nightgown?

I can't say. It was gone in an instant. Maybe a shadow, maybe a wandering cow and calf.

But it sure looked like a woman kneeling over a bundled infant.

Helena's Rowdy Ghosts

OLD HELENA SERVES as a connection to many threads of Wisconsin's past: trade with the lead mining district, way station between Lake Michigan and the Mississippi, home to river boatmen and log rafters, and early immigrant homesteaders.

Helena left behind a reputation as a lively center of commerce. The village was not as tolerant as towns in the mining district when it came to the loud, boisterous, and sometimes violent behavior of the mostly young male pioneer population.

One can easily imagine that the hardworking people of Helena might have run rowdy frontiersmen out of town when disturbances threatened their sleep. Just an occurrence might have led to Helena's "rowdy" ghost phenomena.

This contingent of ghosts has been seen on the outskirts of the former site of Helena—as if they still are not allowed in.

Strangers to the area,—often hunters late in finding their way back to their car,—first think they have stumbled upon a teenage drinking party. Then they see the buckskin and fur caps and the muzzleloading guns. They hear some French accents. They see the revelers take long swigs from jugs and flasks.

Usually these sights and sounds are enough to send the observer off in another direction. Only a few have stayed long enough to observe more horrifying sights.

And we must note that every decade or so someone disappears along this stretch of river-bottom land.

Richard, an Arena area oldtimer remembers the stories: "Young friend of mine saw the ghosts back in the 1920s. He was lost. When he heard the noise he walked right up to them to ask for help. He smelled liquor on them. When he stammered out his request for directions, they sank into a deep chorus of obscene laughter. My friend ran half the night but never looked back."

The oldtimer notes that the incident fit the pattern of earlier tales of a group of drunken traders and trappers. He said there were arguments over the origins of these ghosts. Some said it was an ever-increasing band, added to through decades of frontier fights and river accidents. Others said they all died in one drunken brawl, maybe after a card game, maybe after a dispute over a woman's affections.

"The old men of my boyhood days—you must remember that they were born in the Civil War era and earlier—they said ghosts were most active on what was called in these parts 'Militia Day'. Militia Day is when the volunteers drilled and marched. A band played. There was a baseball game, a picnic, and a keg of beer.

"In the night that followed Militia Day the ghosts would mock the day's activities by drunken marching and singing. They capped it off with target practice on each other! The old man who claimed to have seen it said that they shot at each other at close range.

"Pieces of dead flesh and leather clothing flew away with each hit. But the ghosts just laughed that horrible laugh!"

No one has seen them in the past few years. But several people have heard them on beaches and landings between Arena and Mill Creek.

Linden Mine Ghost

THE VILLAGE OF Linden may seem like a sleepy little community these days. But behind its present look of neat and trim houses lies a rough-and-tumble past.

Like many towns in the mining district, Linden's early days were dominated by immigrants still struggling to fit into the American dream. People worked hard in Linden. And even though the community fell under strict Methodist influence, there was an exuberance to community life.

There were band concerts and socials. There was serious baseball of the Mudville-type immortalized in the poem "Casey at the Bat."

It was in this setting of late nineteenth and early twentieth century community life that the Linden Mine Ghost enjoyed a few decades of notoriety.

This ghost has not been seen for a long time. In the early part of this century this ghost could often be heard pounding a hammer against stones in the southwest side of the village. The oldtimers say that one miner buried another alive and that the pounding was from futile escape efforts.

Supposedly this evil deed took place on the evening after a major baseball game. Team loyalties were at fever pitch and bitter betting money changed hands. Tempers ran high from several questionable umpiring calls that decided the game.

Sometimes winners spent too much time rubbing their victory into the noses of the losers. Some think that may have happened here. Perhaps some heated words were exchanged. A blow was struck, perhaps harder than intended, by the offended party. There was panic and the assumption that the temporarily unconscious miner was dead. The villain took advantage of the night's darkness and the music of a band to transport the body to an abandoned pit on the edge of town.

In those days people pulled up stakes very easily, especially miners. Some would suddenly get a notion to try their luck in Montana or the Yukon. So the victim was not immediately thought of as a missing person.

The hammer tapping was the first clue as to the fate of the missing miner. But no one could pinpoint the source of the sound.

Within a few months the winter set in. It was then that Linden residents first saw the wispy dirt-covered figure gliding along the snowy roads. The ghost seemed to drift on the breeze.

The sightings were commonplace for a number of years. Then in the late summer of 1918 the sightings stopped. Some said that the murderer himself was killed in France on a World War I battlefield at that time. This freed the ghost from looking for his killer.

The hammering is still heard one or two nights in the latter part of each summer. The sound seems to come from the area along the dirt road that leads to the Town of Linden dump. A mobile home park is expanding on this site. Will there be any hammering in those trailers?

Old Graveyard Ghosts of Dodgeville

SOME SAY THAT ghost reports at the corner of Clarence and Union Streets go back to 1828. It was then that the first pioneer burials disturbed an older Indian burial ground. The superstitious thought these early acts of desecration were the cause of later hardships and illnesses in the community.

These earliest spirit sightings were linked to several large trees that bordered the graveyard. Sometimes screaming face apparitions appeared in the gnarly crotches of the trees. Sometimes emaciated corpses seemed to hang from branches and swing in the wind on stormy nights.

The graveyard trees were the tallest objects in the pioneer settlement. Settlers noticed that lightning never struck the trees. Instead, a bolt of lightning would streak toward a treetop and then fork into two bolts, striking the ground on either side of the tree. These errant bolts often singed the graveyard grass and even turned up sod.

The trees stood as graveyard sentinels until the 1840s. Then they were cut down. Legend has it that the last tree felled dropped on the man who ordered them cut down. Supposedly he ended up buried right next to the stump in a box made out of lumber from the tree.

The ghosts at the location became particularly active after construction work in the 1960s disturbed graves.

The Dodgeville graveyard ghosts have a definite social side to them. They are sighted most often after summer evening community events: church suppers, softball games, and July Fourth festivities.

Halloween is also a big time for them. During trick or treating the ghosts join scurrying bands of costumed children and blend right in with the mock goblins. If a child arrives home to discover that his or her pail or bag has less candy loot than expected, well, they might ask whether they knew all their companions.

"The ghosts have a prankster side to them," said Jonathan, a lifelong Dodgeville resident.

"They're quite fond or sticking their heads or hands up through the surface of Union Street to startle drivers and other passersby."

The antics of these ghosts are said to be linked to the large numbers of young people claimed by epidemics in the 1830s, 1840s, and 1850s. They are still working on making up for the fun they missed during their short lives.

This leads to odd courting experiences in Dodgeville.

Even back in horse and buggy days, young people noticed that at times an extra hand seemed to grope in the dark. More than one young man had his face slapped for reasons unknown to him.

On occasion it worked the other way, with previously bashful partners discovering fresh eager lips in the dark along with a strange energy.

When romance moved from the buggy to the automobile, the ghosts followed without hesitation. Cars with steamed-up rear windows were likely to start rocking, or the tires might suddenly go flat. One or two such cars were known to experience parking brake failure and roll down hill.

It is said that the graveyard ghosts also figure in some delicate issues of unplanned parenthood and paternity. Since this book is intended for a family audience, we will leave those details to your imagination.

Pleasant Ridge Peddler

CITY PEOPLE THINK of rural areas as relatively crime-free. And while many of the ghosts of the countryside arise from violent circumstances, that violence is often linked to heroic conflict, tragic misunderstandings, and crimes of passion. Usually there is little hint of thuggery in these stories.

Even Iowa county is not exempt from humankind's darker acts. But it must be pointed out that the most dastardly deeds are seldom homegrown. Rural areas, with their abundance of isolated spots and sparse evidence of authority, often suit the temperament of roving criminals.

Peddlers served as the main representatives of commerce in many rural areas from colonial times until World War II. Their goods ranged from toys to fabrics, from seeds to jewelry, and from books to perfume.

Few peddlers became wealthy men. But in cash-strapped times they were visible targets for robberies and beatings.

In a sense the peddler was the direct ancestor of both the traveling salesman and the convenience store.

Old Isaac was a peddler of the 1860s who traveled a long circuit that started in St. Louis, Missouri, and brought him up the Mississippi Valley to Iowa, Minnesota, and Wisconsin.

Like most peddlers, Old Isaac was an independent businessman. He made his own arrangements to resupply with goods at Rock Island and Prairie du Chien. He hired horses and wagons in areas with established roads and rented pack horses and mules for the back country.

Pete, a freed slave, was Old Isaac's helper and traveling companion. This biracial combination made them a target of scorn and harassment in some quarters. The renegade exconfederate irregulars of Missouri were particularly hateful in this regard.

Many of these erstwhile southern patriots should not have been dignified with the soldier's honor. Many were criminals who took advantage of the chaos of war. The Civil War's end left them mere criminals again.

It was November of 1869 when Old Isaac and Pete set out on their last sales trip of the year.

"I vant to make one trip more to soudvest Visconsin before Vinter," said Old Isaac to Pete.

Five bad men heard of Old Isaac's plan and schemed to rob him. They followed the peddler and his helper onto the riverboat that was going from St. Louis to Rock Island.

Like most criminals, they were not particularly smart. They planned to take Old Isaac's money on the last night of the trip and throw him and Pete overboard. Then, by accident, they overheard Old Isaac ask another businessman to place an order for goods on hold.

"All my money iss in dee gotts I buy already. Vhen I came back, denn I pay."

The robbers cursed each other and drank whiskey for the rest of the voyage.

When the peddler and Pete got off the riverboat the robbers resolved to follow them until there was some evidence of money.

It took awhile for the robbers to steal five horses, so Old Isaac and Pete got a half-day head start up the Rock River.

When the robbers caught up with Old Isaac and Pete, the Peddler had just concluded his first day of brisk sales. They lurked around a river-front store and warehouse long enough to hear that Old Isaac had taken the sales proceeds and converted them into smoked catfish to be shipped back to St. Louis.

So the old man was without money again.

The robbers, now hunted horse thieves, sulked out of town and drank more whiskey by a campfire.

By now Pete noticed that he and Isaac were being followed and he suspected the worst. Old Isaac dismissed Pete's fears.

"Such dumbheads cannot their vay to St. Louis back find. They stop us, denn vee give them some coins."

Old Isaac and Pete gave the robbers the slip several more times. Once in Belmont and once in Mineral Point. Each time Old Isaac managed to convert his sales receipts into goods to be shipped to St. Louis before the robbers arrived on the scene.

In Mineral Point, Old Isaac heard of a cluster of homesteads to the north. There some prosperous homesteaders were said to be good prospects.

He and Pete set out for the area known today as Pleasant Ridge. After some hard travel they reached the cluster of homesteads.

They found warm hospitality and good eating there, but not much in the way of sales.

Old Isaac was philosophical about it.

"Vell, maybe next trip they have money."

All the while the five robbers were lurking in the vicinity.

Old Isaac decided he wanted to get an early start on their return trip. So they rose in the dark and departed from their lodgings in the host's log outbuilding. (It is said that this log granary or toolshed still stands.)

Pete did not feel good about travel before daybreak. But Old Isaac thought the robbers had by now lost interest. He was wrong!

Old Isaac and Pete turned their pack animals south on the rough road leading off Pleasant Ridge back toward Mineral Point. When they reached a low spot in the road surrounded by cedar trees the robbers leapt out. Guns fired and screams pierced the night.

The bodies of Old Isaac and Pete, shot and stabbed, oozed a large pool of blood onto the road. There it mingled with the blood of their two slain riding horses. The robbers cursed their meager booty and rode off with the peddler's pack animals in tow.

Farmers found the bodies the next day and buried them in the cedar grove. The values of the times did not permit burial of a black man in a local cemetery. Some alleged that Old Isaac was Jewish and should not go in a Christian graveyard. But no one was certain of his ethnic background. A low German accent might have been labeled Yiddish. No one knew for sure.

The robbers continued on their crime spree. They were hanged one by one on a trail that led across Iowa, Nebraska, and Kansas.

The peddler's ghost is still seen leading a loaded mule. The sightings are mostly on Highways Z and ZZ, with a few on Griffiths and Davis Roads.

Both the peddler and his animal are said to have red glowing eyes. He and his mule bleed from dozens of wounds and have knives sticking out of them.

Pete sometimes shows up on the road at night. He is always clutching his neck, trying to close a huge bleeding gash.

Somewhere off to the south side of Pleasant Ridge there is a spring by the old trail that will run red on nippy autumn nights. A salty taste reminds one of blood.

Hollandale Wagons

HOLLANDALE CLAIMS A story that is a favorite among drafthorse enthusiasts and antique farm equipment collectors. Local horsemen report hearing variations on the Hollandale tale from as far away as South Dakota.

The wagon legend is varied and colorful. Oddly, very few current Hollandale residents know anything about the stories.

There are so many pieces within this overall legend that we cannot record them all here. The central theme revolves around a runaway team or teams of drafthorses.

Four brothers are the main characters within the legend. They are alternately called the Camps, Kemps, Kamps, or Van Kamps. So their family backgrounds could have been English, German, Danish, or Dutch.

The Camp brothers were young men in the days just before the automobile. Like many young adult brothers, they were high-spirited and competitive. Since they were descended from generations of respected teamsters and cavalrymen, they relished hard-edged competition involving horses. Breaking horses, riding tricks, racing saddle horses, pulling with draft horses, and all manner of farm work. But most of all it meant seeing who could make the best time with a team and wagon between Moscow and Dodgeville.

They did not race at a gallop the whole way. Like long- distance runners, they kept their teams on a pace calculated to give them a burst of energy for the finish. But sometimes they would race right down Hollandale's main streets just to show off.

This practice disturbed the older and more respectable of Hollandale's citizens. And the Camp brothers were the subject of more than one comment from the pulpits of the village's churches. But the young folks of the vicinity enjoyed the sight of the fine-looking animals dashing hellbent for election, nostrils flaring, shod hooves striking up great clods of earth, and the young drivers yelling, whistling, and cracking whips and leaving the town in a cloud of dust (or shower of mud, depending on the season).

Young ladies in the vicinity considered all four brothers as very eligible bachelors. Jake, the oldest, was considered quite handsome with his dark good looks and neatly trimmed moustache. Sam, the second oldest, was the natural athlete and was as equally at home in a foot race, an arm wrestling match, or on the dance floor. George, the third born, had skilled hands that could easily trade horse reins for woodworking tools or a fiddle. Luke, the youngest at seventeen, was a personable young man who could charm with a smooth voice and piercing gray eyes.

Luke, however, suffered the disability of his junior status with competitive chafing. Sometimes he felt that nothing he would do or say could elevate his status in the family pecking order.

The young man tried to break out of his brothers' shadows by greater acts of daring. This sometimes meant a hand-stand on a barn roof peak or a high dive from a cliff into a shallow pool. But in the Camp family it mostly meant some hounds-from-hell horsedriving.

Luke started to take corners routinely on only two wheels of the wagon. Other times he would work his way forward from the wagon seat by walking on the wagon tongue while the team was on the move. A time or two he showed off by starting the team while he ran along side of them, then catch the back wagon gate just at the last minute and pull himself aboard and crawl across the load to the reins.

Finally Luke decided to do something no one In Iowa County had ever seen before. Some say he picked up the idea from a pulp book about Buffalo Bill and the "Wild West" show.

Luke would show his brothers real horsemanship by driving a team while straddled above and between the team with one foot planted on each animal.

He worked in secret practicing the stunt. He was skilled and intuitive when it came to horses. And animals responded well toward him, particularly his gray/blue roan team. His roans were of mixed parentage. Their coloring and powerful legs suggested quite a bit of Percheron blood. But their quickness and spirit hinted at some Arabian cross-breeding. Luke's father, Eli, a good judge of horseflesh, thought that Cleveland Bays and Morgans had also left their mark on the family tree of these gelding half-brothers.

Luke mastered the stunt to his satisfaction after about ten private sessions with the roans. The big gray/blues seemed to delight in the trick and cooperated by delivering a well-synchronized gait.

He then waited for an opportunity to show off his new-found skills.

Soon an occasion arose in the form of a delay in loading Luke's wagon. Four loads had to go to Dodgeville as soon as possible so Jake, Sam, and George set out without Luke.

Luke knew he would meet them on the way back, probably somewhere along Dodge Branch Creek. He would stage his exhibition then.

The last load was finally ready and Luke clicked his tongue and lightly snapped the reins with a "git-up." The roans stepped out proudly and waved their big heads at their excitement at the journey to come.

As expected, Luke ran into his brothers just as the old road started to lift away from the creek bottom and into the rolling hillocks.

Luke spotted them about a half mile off in the distance and developed a plan. He would use an intervening rise and curve as a cover and would dash out and surprise his brothers with his newfound skills.

He and the roans waited beneath a spreading white oak. The roans twitched impatiently. Finally he heard the sound of the oncoming teams and his brothers' loud banter.

Luke moved out and straddled the horses backs. He gave a whistle and the horses moved ahead. He tightened his grip on a short pair of trick reins he had devised for this special function.

The horses picked up speed. The team was showing off every bit as much as their driver.

The older brothers came into view. Their faces were mixtures of anger and delight. They stopped their teams and hooted encouragement and obscenities.

But their expressions turned to horror when Luke lost his footing and fell between the horses. He first bounced on the wagon tongue and tried to hang on.

But the startled team bounced the wagon through a ditch and over some rocks. Luke lost his grip and fell beneath the hooves. His screams further frightened the horses and they bolted back to the road.

Luke tried to get up and out of the way. But the doubletree hit him in the head. Somehow one of the end-iron hooks on the hitch caught Luke's clothing. He was pulled along for more than a hundred yards.

Then the cloth ripped loose. The two right wheels of the loaded wagon passed directly over Luke's head and chest.

He was crushed to death immediately.

The brothers screamed with grief at Luke's bloody and mangled body.

Finally they organized themselves to capture the roan team. Jake started home with Luke's body. Sam and George tried unsuccessfully to calm the team. Finally they transferred the load to another wagon, unharnessed the roans, and tied them behind Sam's wagon.

Luke was buried on the family farm after a well-attended funeral that included a procession with over fifty buggies and wagons.

The Camp family tried to use the roans but they seemed spooked most of the time. Finally Luke's father walked out to the barnyard with a rolling block rifle and killed them both.

A year or two later the good people of Hollandale started to hear a wagon passing through town late at night.

A traveling harness salesman arrived late at the tavern looking for a drink and a room. After his thirst was eased he sought conversation.

"You know, you have some high spirited lads in these parts. I happened to be nearing your fair village—my visit to your blacksmithing and stable establishments the only things on my mind—when out of the night comes a wagon like a bolt of lightening. If not for the moonlight allowing me to find safe haven, my body would surely have joined those of your dear departed citizens in the churchyard.

"The lad in question had a mad gleam in his eye. Perhaps this was only the effect of the moonlight, but the contortions of his face marked him the offspring of hellish inhabitants. Could it be that the youth has been corrupted by local distilleries?"

Such sightings continued at the rate of two or three a year until the introduction of automobiles onto local roads. The chugging horseless carriages drove the ghost wagon from the highways.

Then around the beginning of World War I, Jake died after a prolonged illness.

On the night of his death a driverless team ran past the Camp homestead. Soon thereafter two ghost teams were spotted on the back roads of the town of Moscow and Waldwick.

A few years later Sam passed away. And so a third ghost wagon came to travel the roads at night.

George died a few months later.

Now a fourth wagon joined the other three.

They still run together on lonely nights. Sometimes they are seen as a rushing blur along Highway 191. Sometimes they are merely silhouettes on ridgetop trails.

The Camp brothers delight in pursuing horseriders who are out at night. They also have a fondness for chasing coon hounds out on the hunt.

Hardly any two encounters with the Camp brothers and the Hollandale wagons are alike. Sometimes the wagons are driverless and horseless and moving under their own power. Other times the Camp brothers are seen in their Sunday finery with garters holding up clean white shirt sleeves and derby hats perched on their heads. One sighting involved four skeleton drivers driving rotting wagons pulled by four teams of skeleton horses. The Camp boys still have fun in the other world too—they are sometimes seen chasing a beautiful ghost girl with coppery red hair who rides a shining black mare. The origin of the young lady is unknown.

As the years passed and their contemporaries left our midst, no one could distinguish one brother from another.

Many theories have been offered as to why the sightings vary from ghoulish to benign. The most logical one is that the terror or the satisfaction in sighting spirits is in the eye and the mind of the beholder. Those whose timid minds are dominated by fear of death and by frightening images of a hell populated by goblins and bogeymen will see frightening sights. Those who see life on this earth as but a passing stage and who accept and welcome the fertile mysteries of the unknown are apt to see harmless and amusing images.

So it is that the spirit world evokes the complexity and richness contained within those privileged to brush by it.

One of the most colorful tales of the Hollandale wagons offers evidence of such theories.

The storyteller is a charming old Norwegian-American gentleman. Robert is known to have a vivid imagination within a personality range that allows both for a startled reaction to bumps in the night and for a twinkle in the eye at the telling of a tall tale. His head is filled with "old country" troll stories and he has a fondness for delicate rosemaling.

Here's what he knows of the Hollandale wagons and the Camp boys:

"I heard the stories as a child. I grew up among adults who had seen the ghostly teams.

"It is true that the Hollandale wagons take many forms. I've heard dozens upon dozens of stories. Most were pretty straightforward tales—with young men driving wagons through the night.

"Now I don't for a minute forget that in those days—even with cars commonplace—many farms still had a team of draft horses. So some of these sighting might have been simple exaggerations of actual farm wagons with live teamsters.

"And it might be possible that some of the sightings arose from pranks—youngsters taking old clothes from trunks in the attic and rubbing burnt cork on their faces.

"But I knew of plenty of authentic sightings, too.

"I never saw the Camp brothers as a boy. But I heard them plenty. In the winter time I would hear them just before dawn—whips cracking and horses whinnying down by the road. When I checked I would find faint bobsled tracks in drifting snow. This was on snow-closed roads on stormy nights when no sane person would have been out.

"Then in summer I would hear them up on the ridge. First I would hear hooves striking the stony ground up there. Then a flash of lightning would brighten the ridge. There would be movement in the shadows but nothing clear. Then would come horses snorting followed by thunder. And the pattern would repeat itself.

"I was a young man when I finally saw them for myself. It was the most memorable experience of my life—don't tell my wife and daughters I said that.

"I was driving back from Dodgeville—from a band concert, I recall. We had culture back then, you know. It was my first car. No, not a new one. More of a delivery truck, sort of a half car with a wooden deck on the back.

"It would be a few years until I met and married Ida, so I was still living on Dad's farm. He did not like me visiting town girls in Dodgeville and driving home late.

"The sweet lips of a young German girl kept me in Dodgeville too late. I wanted to get home before Dad got up for milking. So I hurried the car along across the bumps and ruts.

"It was about two miles east of Hollandale that the first sign of something amiss caught my eye. On a looping curve I happened to glance back toward Dodgeville and saw what looked like a line of swinging and bouncing lanterns.

"Every ten seconds or so I looked back and saw the lights gaining on me. I could not understand how this could be since the fifteen miles per hour I was driving was just about the top limit for a rough road at night.

"Then they got close enough for me to see the horses in the glow of the lanterns. Four wagons and four drivers!

"Foolishly, I tried to escape. My poor old car bounded and lurched over the ruts. Loud growling laughter roared close behind me like an explosive blast out of a mine portal.

"One by one they pulled their teams beside me and then passed me. What a sight—a sight I'll carry to my grave!

"Each wagon basked in a soft glow that started with a bundle of St. Elmo's fire on the wagon tongue. Each rider sat on a coffin seat and rested his high polished black boots on a footrest of skulls.

"Snakes of all kinds made up the reins, the harness and collars. The manes and tails of the horses were also snakes. And the drivers carried snake whips.

"Each wagon carried a load of horse bones—skulls, ribs, and leg bones. Each wagon had skull lanterns lining its sides.

"Each driver was finely attired in a black suit. As they passed me, the first three gave me polite smiles and a tip of the hat. The last one flashed a big grin and tipped his whole head!

"That had to be Luke!

"When they were past me they kicked into high gear. Electric sparks showered off the hames and the wagon wheels let down a trail of flame and smoke.

"Then a black fire-rimmed hole opened into the hillside and the teams leapt into the ground. They were gone!

"I never saw or heard them again.

"But if you are driving on Highway 191 late at night be careful. Especially on those moonless overcast nights when the moist fog drifts over the road from the creek bottom. The road is quite curvy. If you are tired and your eyes start to feel heavy, you may be startled to see horses and wagons rounding a curve with sparks jumping off their hooves with each impact on the pavement.

"Suddenly it will be foggier too—with huge clouds of steam billowing from the horses' nostrils as if they were old time locomotives.

"When you see the car and trucks in the ditches along Highway 191 you will know that drivers encountered the Hollandale wagons.

"But don't laugh at those poor drivers. Just around the next turn a surprise awaits you!"

Haunted Mill Creek

GHOST STORIES USUALLY possess an almost comforting level of uniformity about their central characters and themes. But as the introductory "Winny Beaujeau" story suggests, complications arise when the thread of one story leads to another and another.

The tales of Haunted Mill Creek fall into this confusing territory. There are deep disagreements over the identity, location, and behavior of the ghost or ghosts in question.

Like "Winny Beaujeau" there is also a linkage to non-ghostly folklore. In this case a connection to the so-called Mill Creek Hermit.

As I have explained in other stories, the Mill Creek Hermit is a folktale told in at least four distinct ethnic versions: Norwegian, Irish, German, and English/Yankee.

Mill Creek ghost stories seem to share these ethnic variations but vary widely on the role of the Mill Creek Hermit. In some, the hauntings are attributed to the Hermit's ghost. In others the ghosts are victims of the Hermit's revenge. In a few the Hermit is simply a supporting character added for the sake of local color.

Dozens of variations exist from the headwaters of Mill Creek on Evans Quarry Road to the mouth on the Wisconsin River at Tower Hill State Park. The stories are wildly different and often contradictory.

The sources agree only on one fact: Mill Creek is haunted.

My storytellers here were numerous and yet reluctant. There was no "snowball effect" or safety-in-numbers benefit derived from letting them know others were talking, too.

The result is less of a fleshed-out story than a collection of snapshots.

🔥 🔥 🔥

Much of the Mill Creek Hermit story focuses on the north end of Evans Quarry Road. So it should come as no surprise that ghost stories tend to cluster there as well.

One long-time resident makes a direct connection to the Hermit. "It's the Hermit's ghost!", George asserts.

"I've seen him on nights of the full moon. Right on the top of the flood control dam. Hunched over and howling.

"My Grandfather saw him, too, near the same place. But that was long before the flood control dam.

"Grandfather said the ghost was wailing from the murder of his mortal body. The Hermit was a sorcerer, you see. He had magic to keep him from harm.

"But he was a hunchback, too. Magic did not protect his hump even though to touch it was good luck for others. Robbers got a lucky shot and the bullet went through the hump and into his heart.

"The robbers took his gold and buried him under a big rock on the hill to the east of where the ghost is seen. Grandfather told me to steer clear of that rock at night or that souls would be exchanged and the ghost would be in my body."

It is not uncommon for city people to fish Mill Creek because of family ties to the area. Mill Creek offered some fairly diverse fishing before the droughts of the late 1980s: some hefty brown trout, some scrappy brook trout, some smallmouth bass, and even a few holes with bluegills and crappies washed down from Governor Dodge State Park.

One Milwaukee salesman has been coming back for thirty years. "I fished this creek when we visited my Great Aunt when I was a boy," Alan began.

"That was over fifty years ago. My older brothers taught me to fish and we went skinny-dipping right in the hole at the bridge where the two branches meet. My Great Aunt told us about a 'crick ghost'. Only the way she said it, it came out 'the grick ghoost'. She had it all tangled up with trolls, elves, and demons. I think half of her stories were lifted straight from Norwegian stories. She claimed the ghost lived in a cave up off Ridgeview Road. She saw it when she was a girl walking back from the neighbor's farm.

"When I got older I could tell there was a suggestion of the ghost standing in the mouth of the cave doing something obscene or suggestive. She was a proper Victorian lady and it might have been a minor thing. But she was not about to give the details. Who knows, the ghost maybe mooned her.

"As much as she warned of it, we never saw the ghost as kids. Oh, once in awhile somebody would say somebody saw it.

"But then about twenty-five years ago I started bringing back my kids to fish. It worked out that the pool below the dam spillway was a good place to take kids. They could always catch a chub or sucker in there.

"About then the trout started to make a comeback. So I sort of got the bug to wet a line myself. I would come by myself either in early morning or in the evening while the family was visiting relatives in Ridgeway. In those days I was usually the only one fishing the creek.

"One evening I was fishing the spillway pool, just watching the fireflies and listening to the whippoorwills. I was really done fishing but I couldn't bring myself to leave.

"Then what did I see but a stooped-over man in old rags stomp out to the spillway edge. Yeah, right out of the tunnel. He was startled to see me and the sight loosened my bowels! There was a green glow in his deep, empty eye sockets. So don't tell me I didn't see a ghost."

🔥 🔥 🔥

Evans Quarry Road has drawn a fair number of newcomers to its hidden side valleys. As a result this headwaters area of Mill Creek boasts a collection of summer cottages, retreat centers, and housing cooperatives.

Most of these newcomers and visitors are drawn to the scenic beauty. But a few sense the magic that lies just below the surface.

"There's something about the valley that seems mysterious," confesses the lady friend of a weekend cabin owner.

"I'm not fearful of the feeling. It's not frightening. It's a bit intriguing. The feel of the past and the feel of the lives of those before us. And the feel of things close to the Earth.

"You may know that certain times bring a drifting fog down the valley. I've seen a spirit ride the leading edge of this misty tide. It was a beautiful sight."

🔥 🔥 🔥

Many Sunday drivers maintain that the southwest Wisconsin "feel" finds excellent expression in the aptly named Pleasant Valley along Davis Road.

A farmer in this valley knows more then he will tell about the haunting of Mill Creek. He is reluctant to attract attention to himself or to the area.

Prying and pestering brings out but one piece.

"Yes, yes, there's a ghost on the creek," Samuel allowed with resignation and irritation. "I saw him come down riding a raft on high spring thaw waters. Late at night when a steer was crying down in flooded pasture. Didn't that old Hermit tie somebody to a raft in a flood? Maybe that's it."

🔥 🔥 🔥

Hyde Mill gave Mill Creek its name and added to its picturesque flavor.

The mill draws photographers, visitors, and youthful fishing expeditions. The nearby Hyde general store offers cold pop and a glimpse at pre-supermarket shopping.

Mill stories are firmly entrenched in the oral history of all longtime Mill Creek families. In the years between the Civil War and World War One, area children anxiously awaited trips to the mill as highlights of the harvest season.

Stories of ghosts around Hyde Mill draw upon these traditions. But the passing of those harvest grain milling generations leaves fewer details and only one firsthand account.

"I'm the only one who's seen it in the last fifty years," claimed the scrawny fellow in the old Ford station wagon filled with fishing tackle. "But I've made a point of collecting all the stories. Yeah, they'd come if you sat on the porch of the Hyde store long enough back then.

"One of these days I'm going to write a book, so you'll just have to wait and buy it if you want all the details. But I don't want to discourage you, so I'll let you know a little of what I heard from the old folks.

"First the stories had a lot of connection to people on the branch of the creek that runs up Irish Hollow. We're talking about the Pike's Peak Road area. There was a lot of Irish connection in the story. Everything from how the ghost came over in a trunk or in a whiskey jug to how the ghost was a fugitive from the Irish courts.

"Supposedly this fugitive killed an English landlord. Then he came to America and settled right in Mill Creek valley. He lived in a hidden shack.

"It gets a bit hazy after that. There's some talk of murder of the fugitive. Some of a tragic accident.

"Then there are differences about where the ghost resides. Some have him in the mill. Some—actually most—have him under the waterwheel. Others have him in the pond or under the bridge.

"And there are differences in his looks. Some have him in rags. Others in a fine gentleman's coat. Some have him handsome. Others describe him as hideous. And others have seen him as a shapeless, faceless thing. That's how I've seen him. He's a green glow in the dark with only the faintest human outline.

"I've seen him at the mill windows. There was nothing said by words. But he put in my mind that he was waiting for someone to come back.

"It surprised me to see the greenish glow outline of a person. No face or features. It wasn't scary. No, there was something oddly comforting about it.

"But it sure wasn't like the tales they told in the old days. Stuff about a spirit that would get you if you messed around on the wheel or the dam. I half thought it was the way old people had of keeping us kids away from things that would hurt us.

"But I wouldn't mind seeing the green fellow again."

🌿 🌿 🌿

Coon Rock was the name given to an area along the last stretch of Mill Creek, just where its northward flow makes an abrupt turn to the west. It is hard to find much in the way of Coon Rock history. Local people differ as to whether it was simply a name for a landmark or the name of a long-lost hamlet.

A beef farmer on nearby Highway 14 theorizes that Coon Rock and the Mill Creek Ghost are intimately connected. "You might say that Coon Rock was a suburb of old Helena," Philip laughed.

"And a one-resident suburb at that. An old hermit lived there. An old boy out of Maine. A trapper by trade.

"That's where the 'Coon' name came from according to some. Though I've heard many different stories on that. Everything from a flat rock on the crick where coons washed to some long gone boulder that looked like a raccoon.

"But I heard from somebody I believe that the old boy dried coon hides out on a rock. Sounds about right, doesn't it?

"The ghost part comes later. Trapping use to be competitive. It was a good cash crop in the country at one time.

"Some local roughnecks wanted the old Hermit's territory. So they decided to beat him up. They went too far though and the old boy died.

"Then they weighted his body down right where the Coon Rock Road bridge crosses the creek. Then they stole his hides and traps.

"But they never caught much themselves after that. And one by one they disappeared. The old hermit trapper's ghost got them.

"So the haunting mostly comes right at the bridge. Almost always in the night fog after a rain. Sometimes there's splashing in the water. Sometimes there's steel traps clanging.

"When I was a boy I trapped there too. And one frosty morning I stumbled out in the dark to see an old man walking my trapline and robbing my traps. I ran after him and he got away.

"When I got home I told my story, Grandpa said, 'boy you was robbed by the ghost!'"

☙ ☙ ☙

Tower Hill State Park is named after the historic "shot tower." The deep vertical shaft through the rock of the river bluff is not what visitors expect from a "tower."

A considerable amount of Iowa County history revolves around the shot tower, its past operations, and its past owners and operators. Despite popular misconceptions about how exactly lead shot was made at this facility, the site remains a curiosity.

A park volunteer finds considerable interest in stories about the shaft. He also finds that the interest is equally divided between technical appreciation and suspicions of mystery.

"Yes, we get the *Popular Mechanics* guys and the people who just intuitively know that there's something spooky about the shaft," Adam explains.

"They don't like me to tell about it here at the park. It's not DNR policy to recognize ghosts. Even though they've got them at quite a few parks.

"But thirty or forty years ago the story was often told in Spring Green. I guess there was a rash of sightings one winter. Winter is the time when this ghost is active.

"There was a time when those young people with Frank Lloyd Wright would come to see the ghost. But it turned into a circus and I don't think anybody saw anything for awhile.

"The tale I heard said an old German hermit was thrown down the shaft and was killed. Only he didn't die right away. He laid there moaning for days.

"So people would see his ghost at the mouth of the horizontal tunnel that leads to the vertical shaft. It comes right out on the bank of Mill Creek. The ghost was said to be calling for help.

"Now I happen to believe this is one of those ghosts that only certain people can see. I guess you have to be sensitive enough or receptive enough.

"I think it's a skill that people are losing. TV and video games have pretty much dulled our senses.

"But every once and a while we'll get a young child. Somebody who's a first time visitor without knowledge of the story. And they'll just blurt out 'why is that man crying' and point at thin air. I get a kick out of that type of thing.

"Unfortunately I never have experienced that part of it. I only get the horrible sound part. When I visit in the winter I hear terrible screams. The screams of someone falling in a deep hole. It's bone-chilling!"

Ridgeway's Old and New Ghosts

THE TALE OF the Old Ridgeway Ghost is known well enough to give storytellers pause. After all, how many different spins can be spun on that old pioneer legend? Yet closer investigation yields hints of surprisingly diverse sightings of the Old Ridgeway Ghost. The evidence suggests the patterns of pioneer days continue to the present.

One can readily detect that the Old Ridgeway Ghost is a creature of cycles. The sightings peaked in the 1850s, the 1890s, the 1930s, and the 1970s. The majority of the old references focus on a murder victim from a pioneer tavern brawl. The stories often refer to a card game argument that got out of hand.

But it is not simple sorting out the facts from legend nor the Old Ghost tales from the New Ghost tale. The task is even more daunting because Ridgeway's ghosts are fully integrated into the community's boosterism and civic pride. The appearance of a ghost icon on the municipal water tower leaves little doubt that we are dealing as much with a village mascot as a pioneer apparition.

The confusion tends to spill over on to the New Ghost as well. Traditionalists portray the new sightings as simple expansion of the Old Ghost's repertoire. New Ghost advocates point to an entirely separate lineage.

What's a ghost story collector to do except let the two sides tell their versions?

ⱴ ⱴ ⱴ

The farm wife from up on County H is something of a custodian of local history. She differs from most sources in that she has organized files of press clippings, photographs, and correspondence.

She is eager to put the Old Ridgeway Ghost in its full historical perspective.

"You have to go way back," Lizzie warns.

"Way, way back to the old territory. Possibility to the late 1820s when the settlers first started poking around here.

"You had this belt of little communities. Well, really just trading posts, taverns, and stage coach stops at different spots along Military Ridge between Blue Mounds and Ridgeway. Some of these were just huts or log cabins.

"They came and went. Some abandoned and some burned down. Or sometimes things moved to get closer to a spring. This was the pattern for all the little hamlets of the area. Places like Adamsville, old Blue

Mounds, Jenniton, Middlebury, and Pokerville. Ghost towns you could call them.

"No one knows for sure how the ghost came about. And it's no answer to talk about the card game killing. Those were pretty common in the strip of taverns that once existed between Blue Mounds and Ridgeway. One killing for sure in an old log tavern just to the west of the village. But probably at least a half dozen more in the neighborhood, including one at Pokerville as late as the 1850s.

"Then there are all the reports of bad things that happened at Fort Blue Mounds in 1832. Drunken fights with men killed including two Winnebago Army scouts killed by accident.

"But during the 1850s it was the mutilated murder victim that was seen along the Ridge. Mostly it followed travelers. Then around World War One the appearances are different. Less chasing around. More in the way of eerie sounds.

"Many things may have played into these changes. Or, looked at another way, maybe it just shows there was more than one ghost. There was a series of big fires. Three times Ridgeway totally burned to the ground. The first one and the big one was in 1910.

"No local people burned, that we know of. But there was always the ugly rumor that a tramp burned up in a stable. Some think his ghost caused the other fires.

"Then there were the tales connected to the railroad. Some were stories about big wrecks on the Chicago and Northwestern. We had quite a few Ridgeway men who worked on the railroad. And we had someone hit by an express train. So there could be another ghost.

"Around the same time we had all the trouble at St. Bridget's. First there was the noise in the church. Some said it was screaming, others said it was singing. Later it was strange green lights in the church cemetery. Balls of light that came right up out of the graves. Some of it said to be like those UFO sightings.

"Finally came the things at the old parish house. Doors flying open. Window panes falling out of their own accord. All of that was pretty much routine for Ridgeway. Then came the blood.

"Yes, the dripping blood on the parish house staircase. It would just start dripping sometimes. People came from all over to see it. But the

Church was not too enthused about all the fuss. There was talk about an exorcist.

"Anyway all those old things settled down for a good long while. But it must be said that children weren't inclined to roam after dark for many years.

"When the Old Ghost perked up again it was back to following people. But it was now on a white horse that came out of the old mine entrances. And now he was headless.

"People started to notice he was sort of an omen. Some said he was seen just before a death in the community. One man saw the ghost the night before the Barneveld tornado. In fact, a sighting is almost always a sign of bad weather.

"You might think that the Ridgeway Ghost has become too commercial. What with the festival and the lit-up haunted house. But people like their traditions. That's why many of the older people don't like the idea of this New Ghost."

🔥 🔥 🔥

Those who have seen the New Ghost have little patience for pioneer stories. Their ghost has a direct connection to their current lives.

If you want to hear this thoroughly modern tale, drop in a Uncle Milt's Bar and look for a hulking man with a red beard and black leather jacket. For him this is no mere new ghost—it is the Biker Ghost.

🔥 🔥 🔥

"The Biker Ghost was an undercover cop. He was snuffed for pulling a narc number. Set up for an accident with a 'mickey' in his drink. Killed on a big oak tree and became a tortilla man. Well, we gave him a biker funeral anyway.

"But the whole deal comes down to the fact the stories always turn to the bike, not the ghost. We did a ride back over to Pine Bluff. When we sat down for a cold one what was the first question the locals asked? What does that ghost ride?, always starts the jabber when they see we're from Ridgeway. Heard that a hundred times.

"Now you'll hear different versions on this too. Hey but what the heck. I suppose a ghost can have a different ride every night of the week if that's his thing. So I'll just stick to what I saw.

"The ride I saw the Biker Ghost on was a low '55 panhead. You know, with the alloy heads and hydraulic lifter. It's a classic custom job. Restored hydra-glide front forks. Springer fenders and brakes. Ness bits and mirrors.

"It can get up and scoot too. My old grease monkey ear can guess the insides of that ride: inch and three-quarter belt drive in a full cover cage, andrews cam, manley valves, s and s manifold, and a barnett clutch. Easy on the eyes too. Even though I only saw it in dim light. The look of his ride is just what you'd expect for a ghost.

"I've thrown some paint in my time so I have a guess on how it was done. I'll bet it had a silver pearl basecoat with flames put on with a gray pearl basecoat. A great ghost-flame effect.

"It's a biker dream to make a run with the Biker Ghost. I know some who claim they've done it. But most of us don't expect to make that run until after our funerals. That's right, the Biker Ghost runs one hell of a hog rally for dead Harley pushers. I've seen it. Right down Ridgeway's main drag.

"One night I came out of Uncle Milt's Tavern and passed out in the bed of somebody's pickup. When I woke up it sounded like every hog in the world was headed down triple H off of Highway 18. Then they came into sight. Choppers, high performance jobs, wide glides, bad dogs, sportsters, sidecars on electra glides, and FL police models. Each by the hundreds.

"Even little squadrons of WLAs and WLCs driven by World War Two soldiers. The American and Canadian armies had Harley motorcycle units. Plenty died in North Africa and Italy. Here they were riding with blood-soaked bandages.

"It was quite a parade. Like a weird version of Marlon Brando's 'The Wild One.' Skeleton riders. Mutilated riders. Headless riders. Riders with their guts trailing behind them. Leather jackets. Club colors. Clothes in tatters.

"Even one big old fellow on a Honda Golden Wing. Can you beat that?

"I'll bet everybody in North America who ever died on a hog was in that mob of ghosts.

"When they had almost all driven past, the Biker Ghost rode right back through them all in the opposite direction. What does he do but stand up on the seat and give me a wave.

"How about that?"

Part Two

Grant County

Potosi's Brewery Ghost

Fading and crumbling brick may be all that is left of the old Potosi Brewing Company, but memories of its brews linger in the taverns and supper clubs of southwest Wisconsin.

References to labels like Potosi Pilsner, Bohemian Club, and Holiday still bring smiles to the faces of oldtimers.

In the days just before the triumph of the big national breweries, the Potosi Brewery Company was a major regional player—even to the point of sending barges of beer up and down the Mississippi.

So it should come as no surprise that there is plenty of brewery lore in Potosi and surrounding areas.

A number of amateur brewery historians were eager to mention the mysterious and even sinister origins of the brewery. They were, however, unable to provide much in the way of concrete details. Their cryptic comments suggested both tragedy and evil. "Bad things happened in there," and "the place has had hard luck," they said.

But pry as I might, I could not get those Potosi sources to be more forthcoming.

Fortunately an outsider was able to shed light on the circumstances as he told me about southwest Wisconsin's haunted taverns and of ghosts associated with drunken brawls and moonshining.

The retired livestock buyer had plenty of occasion to travel in the region and hear odd stories. He rattled off names and locations from Hillsboro to Hazel Green.

Yet he was matter-of-fact about supernatural references. Where others had been embarrassed about open discussion of ghosts, he was barely interested in those parts of his stories. He was more focused on the sociology of tavern life contained within the broader tales.

"There was a long-ago murder at the brewery," Fred asserted.

The facts were jumbled. No, not in the current building, but in an earlier brewery on the same site. No, it was not a notorious crime; it was covered up as an accident or suicide or maybe the body was hidden. And maybe the ghost had been connected to other weird happenings—no that was another story.

"There was something about the first owner getting bumped off by the people who eventually took over the business," he mentioned, almost as an afterthought.

He remembered that there was some dispute over the direction of the business. Something about a conflict between an English owner and the German brewmaster. He then digressed into rather lengthy speculation about the negative aspects of mixed ethnic businesses.

"Naturally, the German won this particular test of wills," he said by way of return to the topic.

"At least in the short run, for the dead Englishman came back to haunt him. And haunted the business right to the end."

The story further involves a series of business developments. New marketing arrangements, new brewing equipment and company reorganizations fill out this side of the story.

Each new development brought greater success to the business —to a point. Odd equipment failures and sour batches would occur just as new orders were to be filled. Whole railroad cars of beer barrels disappeared. Brewery workers blamed the Englishman's ghost. This drove the German crazy and he would sputter on about stupid Americans. Yet there were indications that the German believed more in ghosts then he let on.

"The old German brought in a priest to exorcise the brewery at night," intoned the retired livestock buyer.

"The way I heard it told, the priest ran out of the brewery wet and smelling of malt. The old German cursed the ghost in English, German, and Latin. The brewmaster seemed even crazier after that."

The story takes another twist here.

In due course the German brewmaster followed the path of all mortals and passed away. It was not long before the German's ghost was haunting the brewery, too.

"The German kept chasing the Englishman around the brewery at night in a noisy ghost race," our source explained.

"He never did catch him. They just went round and round. Not every night of course. But at least four or five times a year people would see this through the brewery windows.

"This went on for years until the brewery finally went belly-up. At that point the ghost of the German brewmaster left the brewery and went to haunt those who had run the brewery into the ground.

"But the Englishman's ghost continues to inhabit the old brewery. I've met a few people in the bar across the street who've seen him regular for the last twenty years.

"Oh, they laugh a little about it. Make bad jokes like, 'It's a brewery spirit—no spirits are distilled not brewed.' But joke as they will, they don't go poking around over there.

"I've seen the old ghost only once. I was coming out of the bar across the street. I was having a hard time getting my truck keys. Then I saw him, muttonchop sideburns and all. Face pressed to a grimy window. Boy, oh, boy—did he look thirsty!"

The Manido of Sinsinawa Mound

Spirit legends of American Indian origin abound in much of Wisconsin. The patterns are particularly strong in areas where the original inhabitants could feel a strong "sense of place."

This tradition tends to drop off in the southern tiers of Wisconsin counties. South of the Wisconsin River valley and Lake Winnebago these stories are relatively rare.

Sinsinawa Mound is the only place in the southern border counties where one could find a thriving American Indian tale of a "manido" or spirit. Even here it is necessary to first pierce a veil of European-American folklore.

The physical beauty of the mound and the serenity of the Dominican sisters' community housed there have long made Sinsinawa a fertile ground for stories with spiritual, mystical, and supernatural elements.

In nearby Hazel Green taverns, one can occasionally hear stories of odd happenings and inexplicable phenomena "out at the Mound." Within these stories one detects a hint of old-fashioned attitudes about the "unnatural" aspects of a women-run community.

The local stories often incorporate references to American Indians. But the context is always heavily European and Catholic. American

Indians are thrown in as "color" in a jumble of saintly miracles, haunt-ings, and demonic possessions.

However, one such local tale did yield up a reference to contempo-rary American Indians and their affinity for the Mound.

A former caretaker claimed that American Indian pilgrims still vis-ited the area. "They come to visit with the Mound Spirit," Ronald whis-pered conspiratorially. "They often come on foot. They stay out of sight. They dig certain things up and leave other things behind. Sometimes you can smell little fires."

What was behind all of that?

Chippewa friends told me that the answers to questions about Sinsi-nawa Mound were not to be found in Wisconsin. "Go to Tama," they said.

Tama is the central Iowa site of a Sac/Fox tribal community. It is also the staging area for a variety of broader tribal efforts to reconnect with Wisconsin and Illinois roots.

Few there wish to speak of spirits or ghosts. There is fear that such talk endangers sensitive negotiations on gambling facilities, land acqui-sitions, and economic development. As with most tribes, there is some tension between those with a business orientation and those who are spir-itual traditionalists.

A friend of a friend helped sort it all out.

"So you think you want to know about the Sinsinawa Manido?," asked the man in the pow-wow shirt with mock surprise.

He was close to forty years old, with striking chiseled features. He had a background in education and social services, but was now con-ducting pipe ceremonies and sweat lodges. Jim clearly had one foot in both worlds.

"The Manido is not an easy thing for non-Indians to understand. Some people hear 'spirit' and they think of a Halloween goblin right away. Or they think of heathens worshipping rocks and idols.

"Like your people often say of politicians, 'they just don't get it.' It just goes to show how much work we have to do. People are so cut off from nature and the things hidden in nature. Yet they are hungry for these things and don't know it.

"That's why you have the 'Lion King' explaining 'the circle of life.' Why you have 'Star Wars' letting you experience 'the force.' Or 'Star Trek' showing you the possibilities of an infinitely mysterious universe. The old cultures and their myths are just about wrecked. So you need to reinvent them. Or borrow some. Like ours.

"Let's start with the basics. What is a manido? Where does it fit in the scheme of things?"

The pipe carrier explained his interpretation of the general teachings. How the manido was seen as a spirit within a thing or of a place. It was not exactly the same as a European-American ghost. It was seldom filled with the torment of unresolved conflict.

He also informed me that American Indian spiritual traditionalists were in the process of reconnecting with the spirits of their past homelands.

"Yes, there are pilgrims," he admitted. "We seek out those old sacred places. We go there to fast. To burn sage and smoke the pipe.

"Don't be surprised if we go quietly. The mission is spiritual, not political. After all, some of these places would send a sheriff's deputy as a welcome wagon. I'll bet if the nuns knew I burned sage on the Mound they'd have a priest sprinkling holy water on me to drive out the devil.

"But let's get back to the Sinsinawa Manido. It is an odd case. I had to visit many old medicine men to solve the puzzle.

"The old stories told of this spirit, but in more than a dozen visits I just couldn't connect with it. I don't mean to brag, but I usually pick up on a local spirit—see a sign, hear a voice, or at least feel something. At Sinsinawa—nothing.

"The old ones told me I would have to get serious. They explained that this was an impaired spirit. It was semi-dormant. Kind of hibernating. One old man called it a ghost of a spirit. There's a braintwister for you.

"So the medicine men got me ready. They put me on a three-day fast. Then I did a sweat. Then I went to Sinsinawa and fasted some more.

"On the second night a mouse ran across my foot. I knew I had a sign then. But the mouse just froze in front of me. Hours passed.

"Then an owl came down out of the trees. The owl grabbed the mouse and ate it while he sat in a tree above me. More hours passed.

"A shooting star came right over the woods. Then the owl started to puke. When the first piece of puke hit the ground it turned into a wolf. The wolf ran off.

"The second chunk of puke turned into a bear. It ran off too.

"The puke kept coming and kept turning into all the creatures of the past. There was an elk. Then a buffalo. And all the four-leggeds back to the cave bear, saber-toothed tiger, and the mastodon.

"When the last creature had run away I understood that the manido was the spirit of the old four-leggeds. He is waiting for them to come back.

"The signs say it can happen. Wolves are seen only a hundred miles north. Bears have been seen within fifty miles. The white buffalo was born seventy-five miles to the east.

"He'll grow stronger as they get closer. And as he grows stronger they will grow stronger.

"I know these things because of what I then saw. The owl opened his mouth and instead of puke thousands of ghosts streamed out. Animals and hunters from through all time.

"Then the owl's mouth got bigger and bigger. So big that in the mouth I could see the prairies with the herds of four-leggeds.

"Out of that same mouth I heard a large beating heart. The heart beat so loud and strong that it chills me now to talk about it.

"So go to the Mound and listen for that heart. Then you'll know the Manido."

Castle Rock's Bohemian Ghosts

EASTERN EUROPEAN INFLUENCES are not easy to find in southwest Wisconsin. One major exception is the Bohemian community around Castle Rock in northeast Grant County.

The very word "bohemian" conjures up all sorts of exotic images: radical freethinkers, nonconformists, and amoral hedonists—images that contrast with the Castle Rock reality of pious Bohemian farmers.

My source here originally contacted me to share recollections about Bohemian-American folklore. She was in a skilled-nursing facility in what turned out to be her last few months of life.

In the course of her extensive remarks about the subculture that flourished around Castle Rock and Bohemian Ridge she made several references to the "old country ghosts."

It was the first time I have ever heard about the wholesale importation of ethnic ghosts by immigrant groups.

🔥 🔥 🔥

"The superstitions revolved around holidays and ghosts," Eva said in a wheezy whisper.

"Old people thought they had brought old country ghosts with them. All of them.

"What kind of ghosts? Every kind. The butchering time ghost. The harvest ghost. The hunting ghost. A ghost for every holiday.

"The ghosts all had names. Old Bohemian names that meant odd things. Such as 'Big Nose,' 'Winter Man,' and 'Dirty Pants.'

"There were ghosts attached to every family and to each of life's big events. Personal events like weddings, funerals, and confirmations.

"Some of these ghosts were associated with old chests brought across the ocean. Some old ladies said they had even brought soil from the old country that had ghosts in it. This was dirt from gardens, cemeteries, and churchyards.

"Life around the Ridge centered on holidays. Christmas and Easter were the main ones.

"Christmas was the most important. Christmas dinner was after dark. You were supposed to wait until the stars were out. Places were set at the table for dead family members and the Christmas Spirit.

"The Christmas Spirit was not Santa Claus. And he was not the Christ Child. It was more like the presence of all those good feelings in all the Christmastimes that had gone before.

"Christmas dinner started with holy bread from church. Bread dipped in honey. With pieces on the spirits' plates. Also, you saved some honey bread for the cows if you wanted good milk in the next year. It was also the night that the old ladies made their tonics. Home remedies, I guess you would call them. And the medicine spirit got a little of each batch.

"Dances were special times too. An old man would play a ghost song before and after the dance. It was supposed to make the spirits happy. Sometimes another old man would pretend to be dancing with somebody.

"This music was different. It scared some children. It was played on a bagpipe. But not on a bagpipe you would know. No, it was a bagpipe made from a whole goatskin, with head, horns, and hooves still on it. The music was supposed to be real old. Maybe a thousand years or more. Who knows?

"But the ghost music was something you'd never forget. When it was played at the end they would turn the lights out. Maybe leave one lantern on. Then you could feel things move in the dark.

"Baking had its ghosts, too. We had big stone ovens. Each year the stone oven was put together on a different farm.

"Good bread came out of those ovens. There was an oven spirit that helped with that. The old ladies put bowls of grain and yeast out near the oven overnight. The oven spirit kept the evil spirits away.

"Yes, we often saw the spirits and ghosts. Sometimes they were little people like the Irish have. But sometimes they appeared as rough-looking dogs.

"Ghosts and spirits are not to be treated like mice or ants, not something to spray or kill. Oh, maybe once in a great while a bad one would get loose and you must fetch the priest. But, most times you would want them around for help.

"So all this being scared and worrying is not something the Bohemians did. Our ghosts were like . . . what's the word? Yes, guardian angels. And our spirits were like watchdogs.

"If you don't keep your spirits and your ghosts, well, then you lose life. Not just community life. It's almost like electricity. A current that goes through all living things."

Mount Ida's Hitchhiker

ROAD PHANTOMS USUALLY stem from long-ago crimes or accidents. Such stories frequently refer to the period of initial pioneer settlement in a given area.

Military Ridge has its share of these tales. They are found in Mount Horeb, Blue Mounds, Barneveld, Ridgeway, Cobb, Montfort, Preston, Mount Hope, Patch Grove, and Brodville.

Mount Ida's highway ghost is different from these others in that he is a thoroughly modern fellow with habits that fall clearly within post-World War Two American culture.

He is called "the Hitchhiker" in recognition of his preferred mode of transportation and his usual method of interaction with the living.

The Hitchhiker is usually described as a young man, somewhere between sixteen and twenty-two years of age. He sports a crew cut and always appears clean-cut even if his jeans and t-shirt have that slept-in look.

He is always seen with his right thumb extended in the traditional sign of those wanting a ride.

Locals seldom pick him up anymore and marvel at those who do. They simply listen to the bewildered stories of strangers who stop to buy fresh produce and tell of a young man who steps out at his destination and seems to vanish.

Many ghost stories exhibit a downward trend in sightings in recent times. The Mount Ida Hitchhiker is an exception here since the frequency of sightings seems to be on the upswing.

The sightings started in 1959 and continued at the rate of one or two per year until 1970. A three-year lack of sightings followed. Then without warning the sightings resumed in 1973 and soon increased to four or five a year.

He is seen along Highway 18 from the west side of Fennimore to the Highway 133 junction at Mount Hope. But he has also appeared south to Shady Dell and north to Werley.

His "home territory" is usually described as that section of Highway 18 between the north and south branches of Highway K. He is seen for hours at a time with thumb extended along this particular stretch of road.

It is sometimes difficult to get people talking about ghostly encounters. They will often resort to a pretense of having heard the story from someone else. In the case of the Mount Ida Hitchhiker, however, accounts of sightings are traded rather freely. It is the background on this spirit that is suppressed by local narrators.

Unlike pioneer-era stories, where the underpinnings are shrouded in the mists of the past, one senses here that the Hitchhiker is literally a skeleton in local closets.

Origins of the Hitchhiker are hinted at only after repeated inquiry. Even the circumstances are alluded to in the vaguest of terms. Each source claims to possess the definitive version and denounces other versions. Conspiratorial motives are attributed to the other versions.

My initial source painted a fairly benign picture.

"The Hitchhiker was a boy who was killed along the highway while waiting for a ride," Charles explained.

"People just don't like to remember the bloody accident. So they connect it to other people who they've got grudges against."

My next source sniffed at that explanation and hinted at a more sinister tale.

"Well, one can't know everything," he offered. "Suppose, just suppose, that a stranger was hitching through the area. Suppose there was an accident. Then think of that time in the Nineteen Fifties. People took care of their own.

"Suppose you have a good local person. And suppose you have a dead vagrant. What purpose is served by raising a big stink? Who's helped by that? "Don't let the people around here fill your head with nonsense!"

The third source was brimming with resentment.

"Be careful of people who are protecting family members" he warned. "Blood is thicker than water. Here in Grant County we can hush up a family secret for a hundred years.

"Yeah, there was an accident alright. But the boy wasn't killed outright. A truck driver got him and a crowd gathered. They all just watched the poor boy die.

"What do you think you would hear from a relative of those who stood around? Do you think that the truck driver's family will tell you the whole story?"

My final source was the most fearful of all.

"I'd be careful poking around in all this if I were you," he cautioned. "You've been bamboozled eight ways from Sunday. Even the coverup story is a coverup for something far worse.

"You need to understand how things work in Grant County. If you're the right person, the D.A., sheriff, and judge can bring themselves to look the other way. Shoot, it's no different than a bunch of Arkansas hillbillies.

"You're not going to get me to say anything directly. It's real easy to get shot resisting arrest around here. "Let's just say I've got some hunches about what happened.

"My crystal ball tells me that the son of a muckety-muck was out cruising with his snotnose friends. On a dare a hitchhiker was run down. I'll bet the poor boy wasn't finished off. I'll bet the snots got out of the car and finished him off with tire irons. I'll bet they hauled the body down to Shady Dell and threw it in a pit and covered it with rocks.

"That's my educated guess."

Conventional wisdom has it that the Mount Ida Hitchhiker is still trying to get out of the area. The locals assume that when he finally is picked up by someone from a family connected to his demise he will be able to settle the score and free himself from this section of Military Ridge.

Spooky Pleasant Ridge

RURAL WISCONSIN BOASTS an abundance of ghost tales drawn from the European-American heritage of its settlers and the interactions of those pioneers with American Indians.

Tales involving other races are few and far between outside of Wisconsin's urban centers. Yet they do exist and a few stick their heads through layers of folklore in southwest Wisconsin. Almost all of these involve African-American stories with themes of runaway slaves and the Underground Railroad.

The stories involving Pleasant Ridge go way beyond the context of slavery. They are rich with the texture of more than a hundred years of African-American life in rural Wisconsin.

It is not generally known in Wisconsin that Pleasant Ridge had a solidified African-American community—with schools, churches, and businesses—long before many Wisconsin cities.

What is odd about Pleasant Ridge folklore is that it lives on mainly in the memories of the community's European-American neighbors. Only a few of Pleasant Ridge's native sons and daughters are still alive. And they are to be found mostly in nursing homes in Milwaukee and Chicago.

As one might expect, local handling of this folklore has not always been gentle or respectful. One hears plenty of stereotypes and more than a few derogatory terms.

But within the ghost tales of Pleasant Ridge one finds universal human themes and hints of affection and respect.

A Beetown resident exemplified this clumsy warmth.

"Darn if I know how you want to talk about this," Jacob began.

"My Grandson told me to watch my mouth. So I don't know if we should talk about Negroes or Coloreds or what. In my Grandfather's day it was Darkies and Freedmen. And of course we've all heard lots worse.

"But I'll just say 'Black' for now when I talk about the people at Pleasant Ridge. I ran with those kids and was raised well by a Black mammy. That's how I know about spooky Pleasant Ridge.

"That's the way the old Black lady who took care of me described it in her stories. She had hundreds of them. And she always ended them with 'that's what you expect on spooky Pleasant Ridge.'"

He presented a long list of odd happenings that were cited by Pleasant Ridge residents as evidence of hauntings and signs from spirits. Some he dismissed and others he elevated to the level of absolute truth.

All the tales brought forth memories of individuals, community events, and seasonal activities. The memories were warm yet laden with the sadness of the passing of this unique rural culture.

He clicked off the families. Shepherd. Brown. Gadlin. Romulus. Wayne. Only echoes on the Grant County wind and names in the Pleasant Ridge cemetery.

He spoke of the community activities. Corn husking. Trips to the sale barns. Quilting. And of a big blow-out festival called the Pleasant Ridge Jamboree.

He said ghost stories had a place at all these events. "You could tell which things were meant as jokes and which were serious," he said by way of qualification.

"There were the ones told by the fire by old uncles and meant to scare naughty kids. There were the ones told by grannies just to teach lessons like Brer' Rabbit. But there were also the ones that made the old people say little prayers. Those were the warning ones.

"Now I'm no college professor. But I'll offer my thoughts on the types of ghosts they talked about. There were four types: murder victim ghosts, old African ghosts, slave ghosts from the South, and ghosts of family members in the cemetery.

"As far as I could tell it was this last type that kept things stirred up. Sometimes the old people would be in an uproar over a ghost of a recently departed person showing up and telling on somebody who took money or committed adultery.

"We had seances. We had gypsies stopping by. We had some phony and some real Indian medicine men stop by. Yeah, some mixed Black and Cherokees out of Oklahoma.

"But then we had two competing camps of people calling on ghosts. We had 'granny doctors' like the old Black Lady that raised me. They were like white magic. Then we had 'conjurers.' They fooled around with devil stuff.

"They did battle with each other. Casting spells and breaking spells. Siccing ghosts on somebody and calling them off.

"All this stuff drove the Brethren pastor crazy. He spoke against all of it. But they just humored him and went right back to it."

He explained how the murder victim ghost was connected to racist acts of vengeance stemming from interracial love affairs. He was also able to give some sparse details on the African ghosts' connection to crops and weather. And he offered lengthy accounts of the slave ghosts.

That was the subject he knew best. That was where he claimed the distinction of personal experience and observation.

"I saw one up at the cemetery. Saw it once as a kid and once just a few years ago.

"He was a big strong man. Shackles still on his wrists, but the chain broken.

"He gave me the biggest smile as a boy—a smile filled with confidence, pride, and a love of everything in this world.

"When I told the old lady about it, she smiled too. She told me to count myself lucky. She said he was a patron ghost just like a patron saint.

"He was the ghost who led people to the safety of Pleasant Ridge. He was the one who watched over them.

"When I saw him last he smiled, but with a touch of sadness. That sadness that says like Moses that he has seen the promised land but will not get there.

"I wish somebody knew how to set him free!"

The Legend of Annaton

GRANT COUNTY LAYS claim to much in the way of early pioneer settlement. The claim is based on unique patterns of Mississippi River migration from the South.

Dozens of early communities formed and disappeared in the years before the Civil War. Many left only names on old maps as their legacy.

A second wave of abandonment came in the latter part of the nineteenth century and early twentieth century as railroad and highway location decisions dictated the fates of communities.

It cannot be said that Wisconsin has much in the way of ghost towns as one might find in the west. Those seeking ghost towns in southwest Wisconsin will not find streets lined with storefronts, creaking shutters, and whipping tumbleweeds. No, they often will be lucky to find any evidence at all of a cluster of buildings.

Abandonment here was a more gradual process. Thrifty farmers cannibalized the buildings to build sheds. Over time even foundation stones were recycled.

Annaton is among those disappeared and dismantled towns. As with so many others there is barely a trace left of human activity or habitation. But Annaton belongs in a different category. It was town of platted streets and substantial houses and businesses, not a pioneer hamlet of temporary dugouts and cabins.

Annaton was also different in the type of story it left behind. The other abandoned towns have their stable ghosts and blacksmith shop ghosts. With Annaton it appears that the town itself is the ghost.

٭ ٭ ٭

Our four sources here are congenial squabblers, contradicting each other and trading lighthearted insults.

They routinely weave fact and fantasy into their recollections of their shared childhood at the Rock School. But on the subject of Annaton the foursome insist on sticking to local accounts and their own experiences.

The two widows and two widowers insist that Annaton exists in another plane and reappears periodically with its structures and inhabitants intact. They even refer to it as "Wisconsin's Brigadoon."

They originally approached the Annaton story as detectives might. Later they developed a sense of warm affection reserved for legends entwined with one's own roots.

"When things seem out of place, you start asking questions and looking for guidance," Mildred explained.

Mildred went on to talk about Eli in Belmont who possessed many photos and letters related to Annaton. She described how her curiosity grew when she discovered that the Belmont man's collection of Annaton artifacts was shrinking.

And she was drawn further into the mystery when Eli dropped the cryptic reference: "Sometimes Annaton's there, sometimes it's not."

Mildred's discovery spurred her companions into action. They soon found many odd things about Annaton's history.

"There was always something odd about Annaton," claimed Bill.

"There were all the rumors about runaways. Runaway kids, runaway husbands, and runaway wives. I realize that sounds pretty tame today.

But back then to leave a family, to leave a marriage, well . . . hells bells, excuse me ladies, you just hung in there until somebody was dead. Or maybe helped along in that direction. But quit? That showed a lack of character.

"Anyway, there was a book—you know, one of those county centennial volumes—that I thought would shed some light on this situation.

"But we had the darnest time finding a copy even though I've seen them for sale at estate auctions.

"So we went to the library. First it was off the shelf. Then we searched the tables and carts. Then it was back on the shelf just before the library was to close.

"So we came back the next day and the darn thing was gone again. This time there wasn't even a card in the card catalog.

"If that wasn't enough, other problems cropped up when we tracked down another copy. There the Annaton pages were missing."

The other three interjected comments on Bill's experiences. They all felt the book problem was insufficient in itself to prove anything. But they allowed how it further spurred their inquiry.

"We thought it was high time to visit the ninety year-olds and hear the story from their mouths," said Rebecca. "We found a lady in a nursing home who was nearly a hundred years old. She was born in Annaton. She was quite feeble, wheelchair bound. Still, her mind seemed alert.

"She told us the most outlandish story about how Annaton disappears and reappears. She feared that she would disappear too.

"She seemed ready to die and face her Maker but was uncertain about being pulled into a place where time, the past, the present, and goodness knows what were all mixed up.

"She explained how, even a century ago, Annaton would temporarily disappear. She said that in the early days such experiences were viewed as insanity. Those fortunate to survive the change usually ended up in their own little room at the county farm. Those who didn't make it through the shift were stuck on the 'other side.'

"She said these incidents gradually increased in frequency until Annaton could not be found except on rare occasions. Annaton's visible time gradually decreased until it could be seen only for a few days a year and then only for a few minutes.

"She suggested that these 'openings' will become fewer and fewer until the link with Annaton closes off forever.

"Then she suggested something absolutely astounding. She said you could use the opening to go back there. She claimed that she knew people who had crossed over. And she said she had thought about it herself but was worried about her need for a wheelchair and medications.

"She claimed that Annaton was heavily populated by real people and ghosts. She believed it was a place where the living could exist physically with their departed loved ones."

It was easy to see that information about the other "other world" made a profound impression on four people whose friends had, by and large, departed this world.

At the time of our first meeting they had obviously formulated a plan. They hinted at their secret intentions as naughty children might.

"We're now in a position to solve this mystery," insisted George. "A chance to go back to a calmer time, a saner time. To do something others only dream of. And to be honest about it, maybe a chance to stop the aging process.

"We experimented a bit. We used a number of clues to figure out when the openings would occur.

"You're not going to get that information out of me. Let's just say that there is a pattern that involves the moon's cycle and a number of other planetary movements. When the conditions are right, there's a place on the hill where the opening is visible. You can see through the opening like a telescope. We even managed to take a picture through there—a photo where the buildings and people where half faded in a mist.

"Yes, we're going to cross over. Nothing anybody can say or do will stop it."

🔥 🔥 🔥

Subsequent meetings filled in more details of Annaton's past and expanded on the foursome's hopes for passage over to Annaton.

After a time they proved impossible to contact. Bill's car was found abandoned on Annaton Road.

Inquiries yielded up different theories. Some thought they had crossed over. Even more thought they were "shacked up" in some retirement community in Florida.

Woodman's Tramp

POLITICAL FASHION DICTATES public perceptions of the poor. One era might produce descriptions of quiet dignity. Another brings forth accusatory moral judgements.

The terms enable us to chart these ups and down: hoboes, tramps, bums, unemployed, migrants, homeless, displaced workers, welfare parasites, etc.

There is a sub-genre of folklore and ghost tales that deal with the poor and their role in the community. Such stories are generally sketchy and reflect the low social standing and anonymous background of the subjects. They are often referred to as nameless hobo ghosts.

Woodman's Tramp is perhaps the most fleshed-out version of such a ghost one could encounter in Wisconsin.

First and foremost he has a name or names: Tim, Timmy, Timothy, and Tim the Tinker. He is also unique in that he stands on his own apart from the typical hobo ghost connection to railroads (or earlier ship-borne stowaway ghosts). Tim is a rural ghost whose territory is quite different from the usual environment of rail yards, warehouses, and abandoned factories of other hobo ghosts.

His story cannot be told in the individual storyteller narrative style. It is a shared experience in which five to six oldtimers get to toss in things they saw themselves or heard from older friends and family.

🌿 🌿 🌿

Tim is most often seen on Rosendale Road and Shady Hollow Lane. He is rarely seen outside of the Town of Woodman except for an isolated sighting in the Town of Marion.

Like most hobo ghosts he is a benign character. He is noted for leading lost children home and performing other good deeds.

"He's been known to fetch help in an emergency," one fellow pointed out.

"In one situation we had a tree-cutter who was pinned by a log. It got dark and he would have froze to death. But Tim pestered the neighbors and got them to follow. They found the man in time so he didn't need an amputation."

He is also a patron saint of sorts for tipsy drivers. Since he is beyond further injury, he can perform the service of standing in the road and startling nodding drivers back into a more alert state.

Some people think that a practice of tribute has led such grateful drivers to leave Tim an occasional quart bottle of beer in a Dutch Hill Road culvert. At least the empties are always found there.

"Tim is often seen nursing a bottle," chuckled one confessed barley pop lover. "He has a summer ritual. He drinks his beer laid out on loads of hay. It is said he has a girlfriend ghost that he meets on those summer nights."

There was a time when this ghost was thought to chaperon young couples parked on hidden farm lanes. One wag talked crudely of "ghostus interruptus."

My sources did not deny that Woodman's Tramp had intervened to prevent teenage parenthood. But several were quick to point out that once the salutary effects of such intervention were generally known, fathers and older brothers took it upon themselves to act as Tim's proxies at well-known parking locations.

There was further admission that Tim's activities were expanded on through the intervention of the living in many cases. "In my grandfather's day the ghost herded some cows back to their owner," one source stated.

"It is true that he performed other good deeds. But he also became a symbol of neighborliness. Many helpful neighbors concealed their own good deeds and credited the ghost. A hurt farmer might find his hay brought in. Or a widow might find her house painted. Good samaritans would just smile and say the ghost did it."

There is little agreement about the ghost's origins. The circumstances of his death are the subject of dispute. Links to any local family are uncertain and contradictory.

The theories about his demise are pretty much what one might expect. One school of thought proposes (without a shred of proof) that Tim was murdered for his meager possessions. Another relies on the reported (but out of chronological place with the earliest ghost sightings) incident of an itinerant laborer's accidental death. The final camp builds a case around Tim's death by exposure.

Here, too, there are accounts that serve as a foundation. A farm laborer between jobs was said to have frozen to death in a rough cabin near where Virgin Road intersects with Dutch Hill Road.

Tim's own actions and words support this theory.

While not a single local resident has had a conversation with Tim, he is quite verbal with strangers. The strangers, of course, do not realize Tim's ethereal nature and report the encounters as rescues by an eccentric country bumpkin.

"He has saved several city drivers lost in snowstorms," asserted the retired snowplow driver. "It was pretty much the same deal each time. People with no business out on a bad night would break down or get stuck. Tim would come along and get them through it. Tell them to sit tight. Keep awake. Promise help would come. Even give them old moth-eaten blankets.

"Then he would warn them about the dangers of the cold. Tell them about how he learned the hard way not to mess with winter. Then he would go down the road and pester one of us until we followed. That's how he pulled off the rescues.

"When we would tell those city people about how they were saved by a ghost you could tell most thought we were crazy.

"One kind lady was different though. She came back and left a pile of new blankets at the culvert where we leave the beer. Darn if the new ones didn't disappear and in their place old ratty ones were left behind."

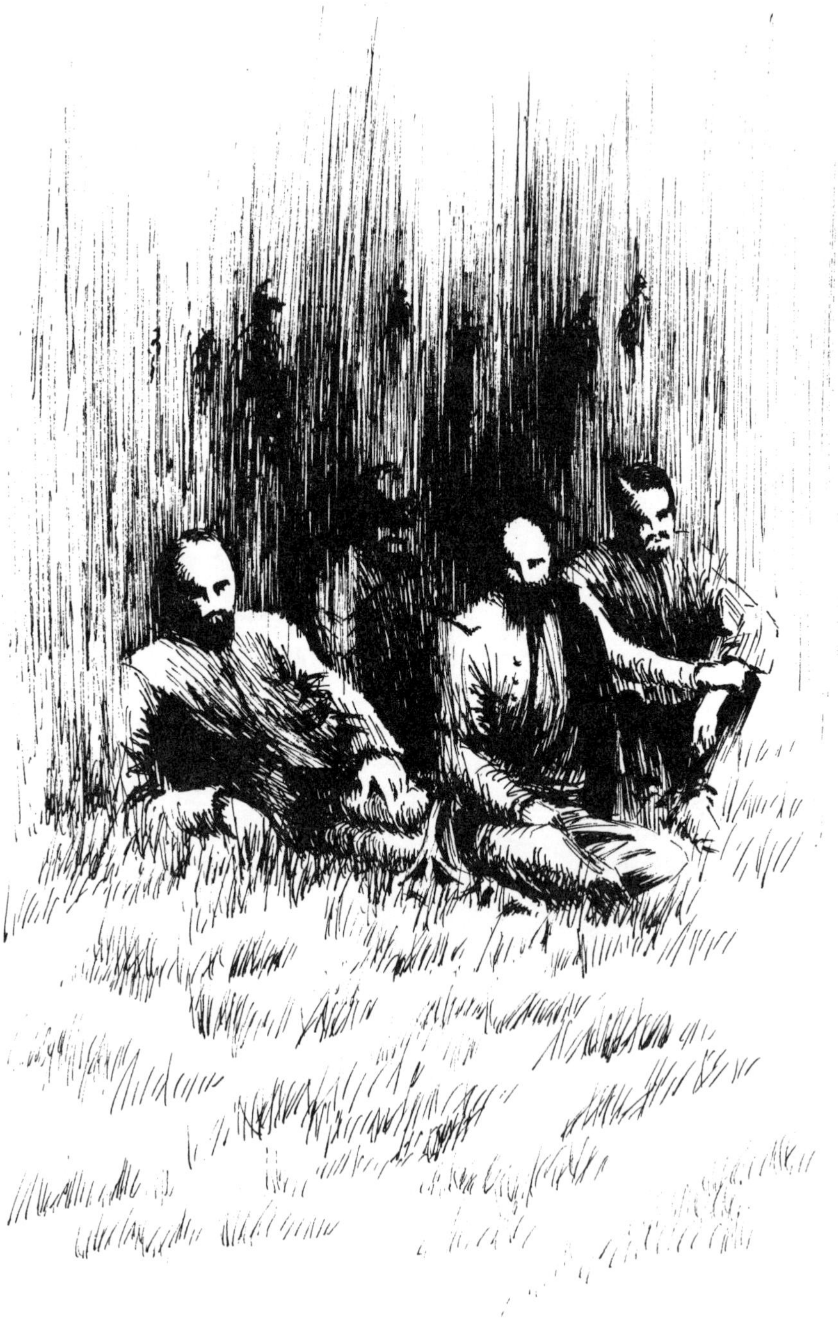

Part Three

Crawford County

Soldiers Grove Phantoms

WISCONSIN WAS FAR from the major battlefields of the Civil War. Such geographical distance, however, did not prevent the emergence of soldier ghosts in country cemeteries and the mustering depots in the southern third of the State.

As is the case with many ghost stories, there are only present day fragments of what were once rich and complex stories involving local personalities and history. Often the story has reduced to a single sentence: "There's a ghost of a cavalryman in that cemetery." Such references can be found by the dozens.

A chance encounter with a Civil War reenactment buff brought many such abbreviated tales to my attention. He also spoke of two more complete stories of this genre.

He put me on the trail of the Soldiers Grove phantoms and the Confederate Prisoner Ghosts of Camp Randall in Madison. Instinct suggested that the well-known circumstances surrounding the rebel prisoners might yield a novel-length story and that the Soldiers Grove reference was obscure at best. Wrong. It turned out exactly the opposite.

The Soldiers Grove story was relatively easy to piece together. The Madison story proved elusive and may not be available for years. One could speculate on the hows and the whys of oral tradition preservation in rural areas versus cities. Instead, I will let Crawford County residents talk about their "boys."

🌿 🌿 🌿

"At one time they were called 'our boys'," recalled Matt, a livestock hauler.

"It was as if 'our boys' had just marched back from war. There was no sense of them being from a long time ago. In fact, many people didn't connect them to any particular war. It was just normal that Soldiers Grove had soldier ghosts."

Most sources explained that the ghosts were not all war casualties. Local conventional wisdom simply described them as comrades who carried out old encampment routines.

"No, no, they're not just the war dead," admonished a Town of Clayton resident.

"I've seen the phantoms three times. One time they were on the march west on Gander Road. The other two times they were camped out along the Kickapoo.

"All this was at night. Always on summer nights close to the solstice. You know, nights where it doesn't really get dark until ten o'clock.

"The first time I stumbled into their camp I thought it was a bunch of Gays Mills hippies throwing a party. You know, beards and long hair and all. But they all kind of faded in and out like Iowa TV stations. When one of them drifted away like steam I hightailed out of there.

"The next time I came upon them I held back and snooped. Darn if they weren't playing cards, singing songs, and nipping at a barrel."

Other witnesses alleged slightly different circumstances. They claimed similar settings of parades and encampments. But this minority view also insisted that each appearance of the soldier ghosts was marked by a jig dance of amputees.

"I'm not kidding," asserted one Montgomeryville resident.

"I saw it with my own eyes. A group of say sixty or so sat in a circle while two fiddlers played music. In the middle of the circle about a dozen men danced herky-jerky.

"That wasn't the half of it. When I got a closer look I could see that some were hopping on one leg. Some were bouncing on the stumps of limbs. Right beside them their blown off and cut off arms and legs danced along. There was even a head bobbing over a twitching pair of boots."

The observers of the amputee dances claimed that such events occur around Memorial Day rather than the summer solstice. There was a general feeling among them that such events followed Memorial Day by a day or two and reflected the ghosts' assessment of whether the holiday was properly observed.

A few witnesses to this variation speculated that the whole phenomenon of the Soldiers Grove Phantoms had little to do with war itself. They felt that the essence of the sightings flowed from the feelings left behind by the comradarie of the Grand Army of the Republic and other fraternal veterans groups.

When I interviewed the Civil War re-enactment buff a second time he had carried his research in a more historically based direction.

He felt that he had been able to link specific ghosts to individual soldiers from Crawford, Vernon, and Richland counties. He had spent many hours at the Wisconsin Veterans Museum and the State Historical Society searching records of the various units of the Wisconsin volunteers.

He told me that he had been able to identify the military companies represented in Soldiers Grove. He was certain of at least four different units.

He also spoke about individual officers, sergeants, color bearers, drummer boys, and buglers as if he knew them personally. He seemed to know their personal as well as military histories.

When I pressed him on this he made a confession.

"After I completed my research I just had to see if any of this went beyond quaint tales," Dan admitted with obvious embarrassment.

"So I journeyed up to Soldiers Grove last summer's solstice. I took along twelve bottles of Berghoff and a stick of venison summer sausage. I had coffeed up earlier so I was set for a late night wait.

"I arrived around sunset. I found a west coast ballgame on the radio and listened to the last three or four innings. Then I picked up a Tennessee country-western station and listened to Hank Williams Senior for a bit.

"About eleven p.m. I got out of the truck and walked over to where the phantoms have been seen. I sat down and opened another beer. Midnight came. Nothing.

"Then I must have fallen asleep leaning up against a tree.

"Noise woke me up. Darn if I wasn't in the middle of a camp! Campfires burning, sentries moving out for picket duty, and dispatch messengers riding in and out.

"I got up and walked over to a group of men around a fire. They welcomed me and gave me tobacco.

"I learned more that night then I had in years of reading books. I learned that the soldiers were just regular people who didn't really want to be in the army.

"They told me stories until the faintest lip of dawn's light appeared in the east. Then a bugle blew. They grabbed their rifles from the stacks and formed up in columns. Without another word they marched into a layer of river fog."

The Devil's Pack

IT WOULD BE a big mistake for a collector of tales to step into any rivalries between the various localities about who boasts the strangest tales.

But the collector's vantage point also permits an overview and some conclusions. Square mile for square mile, Iowa County leads in ghost stories. Grant County has a clear edge in twinkle-in-the-eye tales. Lafayette County stories can echo with frontier fear and excitement. Vernon County produces oddities and curiosities. In Sauk and Richland Counties there is mystery as wide and as strong as the Wisconsin River.

But it is Crawford County that clearly wins on the eeriness scale. Nowhere have I heard as many look-over-your-shoulder-in-the-dark stories.

Something in the water or something in the local character? Only professionals could answer those questions.

It should be noted, however, that Crawford County storytellers often live in deep valleys in houses set into hillsides. This means that they live in shadows a few more hours a day than the rest of us.

This is the setting for our storyteller here.

🌿 🌿 🌿

"Just tell them I live in the Town of Haney in Crawford County," Myron laughed with a gleam in his eye.

"Sure they can drive out this way. Many strangers do. But if they try to find the places in this story, well, they just might get lost. And then they just might break down on a back road after dark. That would be too bad, wouldn't it? No telling what might happen, then.

"I often see strange things. I've lived in this house since I was born and I've seen things ever since I can remember.

"The first thing was right in this house. I was about three years old. I went down the stairs into the cellar when I wasn't supposed to. I saw a hand in a hole in the wall. The hand pushed a stone into place and closed the hole.

"These houses we have out this way are often built into the hillsides. That means the back cellar walls are really part of the hill. With that you often find that the cellar has an artesian well or spring or crack into the rocks.

"Ours here had a little cave that was once used as a root cellar. But it was walled off. Nobody would say why.

"After I got the house—years later—I opened up that root cellar. There are four or five bushels of apples down there now. I haven't seen a hand coming out ever since we opened it.

"I often heard stories like that from people who live in houses like this. Too much time in dark and shadow they say. Not that most of them would tell such things to people they don't know.

"Makes you wonder if our ancestors weren't under mysterious influences when they built these places. Sure it's nice to be out of the wind. But why in these little narrow places?

"They get called hollows, ravines, gullies, crick cracks, coulees, and valleys. But I just call mine an old washout.

"You can get that wintertime craziness in those shadows. Winter seems even longer. I often have snow and ice behind the house until May.

"These shadowy washouts are great places for things that don't like to stand out in the middle of a sunlit field. That's why we're seeing bears, wildcats, and even cougars over this way. Then there are the things that don't have names or where you don't even want to know a name.

"I know a fellow up the road who's cursed with a bunch of those things. A twitchy nervous little fellow I always thought. I thought him odd before I knew what he was living through.

"He never said a word about what was going on. You'd just see him hurrying down logging roads in the shadows. Always looking back behind him.

"It got so I just had to see what was going on. If you knew me well you'd know that goes against my grain. I don't consider it very neighborly to snoop on a neighbor. So I did something on the sneaky side. I crept up on the neighbor one evening. Well, it wasn't real late, the evening star had just come out.

"I thought I heard quite a racket. When I got closer I heard barking. Lots of barking. And the neighbor didn't keep dogs as far as I knew.

"When I got up to the buildings I could tell the sound wasn't coming from the barn or sheds. No, it was coming from the house.

"I looked into the kitchen window and didn't see a thing. The barking started again. Then I knew the commotion was down in the cellar.

"So I peeked in the little cellar window. At first I couldn't see much. The glass was dirty with cobwebs. Then the neighbor came into view with a lantern.

"He opened a small—maybe three by four foot—double-battened wood door. Out bounded six growling, snapping, and slobbering dogs.

"Now these weren't your standard lab pups or coon dogs. They were a vicious lot. Wild looking. Not like wolves or coyotes. No, more like monsters.

"Anyway they weren't hanging around. They busted right out through the slanted walk-down cellar door. I was right alongside there and I put my back to the wall. But they weren't stopping for me. They went up the hill like a shot.

"I looked back into the cellar window and saw the neighbor close the little door in the back cellar wall. I looked closer and could see it was an old root cellar. Probably a cave in the hillside like mine.

"When his face came back into view I could see an expression of pure terror. Not fear for himself, but a sickening revulsion and shame for what he had let loose on the world.

"Over the weeks and months and years spying on the neighbor, I was able to see some patterns and learn a few things about this phenomenon. He didn't let them out every night. Sometimes months would go by without any release.

"He let them out when they demanded it. They would set up such a hellish racket. I guess he didn't have any choice. The barking shook his house and drove him crazy.

"I tried to read up on what this might be, but I couldn't find anything very useful in the libraries. Just some things about mythological dogs. Usually in the form of guardians of hell.

"But over the years I watched the auctions and fleamarkets and found books that shed light on the neighbor's curse. And I mean old books. Ones bound in leather and falling apart.

"One old one was called *Gatekeepers of the Underworld*. It talked about the hounds of hell in all their roles: sentinels, messengers, and dark angels of vengeance.

"Then I picked up other stuff that was half in Latin and had charms and curses. Stuff that was a bit on the wild side if you ask me. Connections to Norse gods and other old European legends. And they rarely had a clear author. Often they would say on the cover that the material was from the collected works of Nostradamus or Albert Magnum.

"But the most valuable source was a privately printed account of pioneer life in Crawford County. It centered mostly around the farming experience and hunting adventures of a Schmidt family that turned themselves into a Smith family. But buried in that book was a story about 'The Devil's Pack.'

"You can bet that caught my eye. I mean how many different packs of monster dogs would you find in one area?

"The book told about some old things that happened to pioneers. Most of which at first glance you could call bad luck.

"But then as I got further into the story I could see some patterns. The 'accidents' seemed to fall into a couple of outside work categories. Mostly logging, wood cutting, and harvest time activities. The last involved mostly horses - runaway teams and such.

"The book also made the claim that the Devil's Pack was quite ancient. Now lost Kickapoo legends were mentioned and attributed to an old Indian who traveled through the area after the Civil War.

"They said that old Indian claimed that he was born in the area before the Black Hawk War. And that he told about how those who tried to go back on deals they made with evil spirits were punished by dog-beasts.

"The old Indian made a number of claims as the Smiths or Schmidts told it. First, the dogs had some regular paths they used. Second, their victims were not random, but were, in fact, guilty of various moral lapses. Third, every time they were set loose there was some tragedy that hit somewhere. And last, there was a definite seasonal pattern.

"Those legends were said to go way, way back, thousands of years. The old Indian supposedly connected the Devil's Pack to the disappearance of the mound-builders and to the mostly uninhabited status of the area.

"They say Indians didn't live here on a year-round basis. They just hunted around here in the summer and early fall. Those who know about those times say it was kind of a no-man's-land for the various tribes.

"So I started tracking all this stuff to see if it checked out. Just to see if there was anything to these stories that would connect with what I was seeing at the neighbor's house.

"First, I looked for any link to the times the dogs were loose and any bad things that happened. And I'll tell you, nine times out of ten, there was a death notice in the paper. Everything from farm bull gorings to tractor upsets to cars upside down in rivers.

"Of course this wasn't happening every day. More like six to ten times a year. And over many years.

"Then I looked at the thing about certain paths for the Devil's Pack. Early on I could see that they went up and down the Kickapoo quite a bit. And as time went by I could tell they had runs on Vinegar Ridge and on Pleasant Ridge. There may even be standard routes up on North Clayton Ridge and down in Tucker Hollow.

"It kind of raises the question about the range of these evil critters. By and large they're a Crawford County problem. But I think they might have crossed to Lansing and Harper's Ferry in Iowa. And I'm pretty sure they made visits to Jimtown, Folsom, and Woodman. The old Smith book names all these routes as old mound-builder trails. Others called them warrior roads.

"As far as time of year goes, it's a mixed bag. It sure worked out that these accident deaths were concentrated in the fall at times when the dogs were loose. But there were other times when the Pack was running when nothing happened as far as I could tell.

"Now it could be that it happened further away and I never heard about it. Or it could be like the *Gatekeepers* book said and they could have been off on other errands for the Devil.

"Finally, there's the matter of the 'who' and the 'why.' I found nothing linking the people together. No hint of them knowing each other.

"With most, there was some suggestion that they had done wrong somewhere along the line. And often as not they weren't exactly missed after they were gone. Their crimes didn't seem big-time on the surface. You never know though, maybe they were axe murderers. So maybe it really was a matter of deals with the Devil over greed, or curses placed on others.

"But as far as I could see, it was either small potatoes or tragic. Stuff like a fellow fooling around with his brother's wife. Or someone who used shady bookkeeping to get the upper hand on the farm credit people. Hell, that's almost a heroic thing.

"The tragic thing involved a fellow who cut and ran on his buddies in World War Two. They were wiped out. So he had to live with that for over forty years. That would be punishment enough, you'd think.

"The *Gatekeeper* book gave a possible answer. If I understand correctly, there's sort of a quota for souls. So if there was a shortage, the Pack would take whoever was available.

"It's a scary thing. I mean, everyone has something that they shouldn't have done. I guess that applies to me, too. I've had this feeling that one night they'll come for me. I'm not a bad man, I don't think. But like so many others, I have a secret.

"If they come—when they come—I guess I'll find out the whole story on the Devil's Pack."

Ferryville's Witch

HIGHWAY 35 ALONG the east bank of the Mississippi River is one of Wisconsin's premier drives. The scenery has a full four seasons to delight the eye with eagles wheeling above and fish jumping in the coulees.

Among the sights worthy of sample are the strip towns that dot Highway 35. You can find them where the hills crowd the riverbanks and create communities that are only one or two houses wide.

Floods notwithstanding, there is much to envy about villages where each dwelling is blessed with a good view of the river. Some would say that this feature alone is enough to keep strip-town residents in constant communion with nature.

Strip-town dwellers have their share of stories. Most focus on the natural elements and the rigors and mysteries of the river.

Almost every cafe and tavern between Sandy Hook and Maple Grove can produce a bushel of tales about disappearances of boaters, fishermen, and duck hunters. Many of these tales have an element of superstition to them. In most cases the accidents are explained with a simple "the river got 'em." But even that simplicity suggests an unseen conscious force. In a few places you can hear hints of an identity; vague references to a spirit, a thing, or a monster.

One Ferryville resident does have a name for this force, and ascribes a personality to it.

"... And that's what I heard about that houseboat accident a couple of years ago. They never found that Iowa man.

"Yeah, lots of tourists ask about river stories. I usually get a free beer or two out of the deal. Helps stretch my disability checks.

"They usually want to hear about fishing, the floods, the railroad, or about the old taverns, churches, and cheese factories. Lots of people come just to visit our cheese factory. And I'd put up our taverns against any little town.

"I got one story that's a bit different. Some don't like to hear it. But I'll tell you if you got time."

A pause. Wasn't a nod of assent enough encouragement? Then I remembered the reference to "a free beer or two." I motioned for the bartender to fill our glasses.

A closer glance at this Ferryville storyteller revealed his thin build. He was dressed oddly for a man in his early fifties. A fresh Roy Rogers shirt, pleated wide-wale corduroys, and shiny black oxford shoes—almost like he had dug into an attic trunk to retrieve something he had worn as a boy.

There was something else about the thin man that suggested arrested development, but I couldn't put my finger on it. Maybe it was the transparently eager look on his face as the bartender filled the beer glass. Maybe it was the simple glee that filled his eyes when the full glass was cradled in his hands.

The thin man gazed lovingly at the glass and finally took a long sip. His eyes closed as if he were overtaken by sensuous delights. Finally, he took another long sip. Then he shook his head as if braced by a splash of cold water in his face.

"Ah," he moaned pleasurably, "nothing like a good cold one to give you a new look at the world.

"Where was I? Oh, yeah, my experiences with the evil one.

"Yeah, evil. That's what she was and that's the twisted magic she still works now that she's gone.

"You don't have a clue to what I'm talking about, do you? You think I'm crazy, don't you? Well, I don't give a rat's butt about your opinion, mister. I know the Ferryville Witch. I knew her and I know where she went.

"I don't have to name names. If you ain't from around here it would-n't mean nothing to you anyway. If you were from here then I wouldn't need to tell you unless you were a youngster.

"Everybody over forty knows something about this. We had quite a little scandal going back when.

"If you ask others around here about this deal they'll give you the wrong impression. They'll tell you that my family had a feud with the witch's family. And that's true up to a point. But it ain't got nothing to do with what I got to tell you.

"First off, you need to know that there were other witches in that family. I'd say going back at least a hundred years or more here in Craw-ford County. I heard the family was from Marquette County before that, so I can't say what might have happened over there.

"They lived in different places. They once had a farm up Buck Creek Road. But they were in Ferryville for at least three generations.

"They weren't ambitious sorts. The men cut wood and took summer jobs fixing railroad track. The women mostly took in sewing. They lived in shacks that seemed to get hauled away by floods.

"My grandmother told me that the charms and spells started around the turn of the century. That's when we had an epidemic of married men running off with single girls. Grandma said that the old lady in the witch family had a fondness for married men and if they rejected her she put a curse on them that made them fall in love with teenage girls and wreck their homes.

"When that old lady died, her daughter took over. Then we had sick-ness around here for a long time. We lost a lot of the old people. And we kept hearing about strange little dances in nearby cemeteries at night.

"The daughter of the old lady offered cures for these sicknesses—for a price. And sure enough, when people paid, the disease went away. It also built up a nice nest egg for the daughter.

"The money went into building a regular house for the family. They built further away from the river. They built a little further uphill than anybody else at that time. Darn if the next spring thaw didn't damage everybody except them.

"The daughter was thought to be the source of bad luck during the Depression. If a cow died or a well went bad it was blamed on her. Heck, a barn burned up at Mt. Sterling and people said she did it. Then down in Lynxville she was said to have caused some kids to be swept away on a raft.

"Once a mob from Lansing, Iowa, come over to hunt her down. They said she was behind some drownings over there. They didn't find her because she hid out on one of the islands. But a bunch of government men, engineers and such, planning roads and dams, heard the fuss. They told newspapers. We got bad write-ups out of that. We were compared to hillbillies and hottentots.

"I want to get back to that house they built. If you look for it, you'll see it. It's different. Everybody else has their windows facing the river. The witch house has only one window facing the river and that one is boarded up.

"Grandma said that was because witches don't like water. She said it can kill them and that's why they don't bathe or swim.

"The house also had a room that nobody was let into. It had no windows. And some said there was an organ in there that the witches played late at night.

"By the time I was a kid the granddaughter had taken over the house. She was the one who scared me. She would often look at me out a window with one eye closed and pointing a finger at me. She had it out for me.

"Now we had a retired professor who moved here to be close to the river. He said he had studied strange and evil things. He said two things that I remember. First, he claimed that all the evil things, and witches in particular, only gained a toehold where the good things, like the church, were weak. Second, he said there really wasn't an old lady, a daughter and a granddaughter, but all were one person.

"Now the first thing is probably true. There's a lot more interest in fishing around here than in Sunday services. The pastors don't last long around here. Some even take to the bottle or get caught with the neighbor lady.

"The second thing is harder to understand. I mean, people knew the three women. Yet the old professor said it was really just one witch the whole time. He said they can change their appearances for short periods of time. And they can get younger for quite a while if they steal a young person's soul. Or so said the professor.

"I think the witch got the professor. He went kind of crazy and they put him in a home. That was nearly thirty years ago. That's when things were really bad. The professor was going to bring in some experts to fix her. But he never got to it. It was a bad time for everybody. Lots of bad luck and people moving away.

"She really put the curse on young girls back then. I remember the girls I grew up with all of a sudden acting strange. It started when they were about thirteen or fourteen years old. By the time they were eighteen or so they would just move away to Madison or Chicago.

"It really mucked up romance around here. Plenty of the boys had to go all the way to Prairie du Chien to find a girl to take to a dance. That's why I never got married. I wasn't going to take the chance to get married to a cursed one.

"But the romance stuff wasn't the worst of it. Outsiders started to disappear near here. Boaters from Iowa, Illinois, and Minnesota. Some fishermen, too. Relatives and sometimes police would stop in Ferryville to ask questions about missing people. But there was nothing we wanted to tell them.

"Me and some of the boys thought we would put a stop to it. We were all about eighteen. All soon to graduate high school and go into the service.

"I didn't pass the physical, but the others went. I couldn't tell you where any of them are today.

"We thought we were tough. We played football, you know. Anyway, we planned to run off the witch.

"Everybody knew she took a Friday night walk along the river, though nobody knew what she did down there. Our plan was to follow her, grab her, and shake her up a bit.

"So we followed her down to a place where a spring flows into a backwater made by a sandbar. It's not there anymore. It was a full-moon night so we could see her good. But the surprise came when she took off her clothes and went into the water.

"We were surprised in two ways. First, witches weren't supposed to like water. Second, under the clothes was a young woman, not an old lady.

"Something happened to all of us boys. Magic or whatever. Anyway, we all went into the water to play with her. And after the swim, strange things happened on the sandbar.

"One by one she took the boys behind a bush. You can guess the rest. I was the only one who didn't go behind the bush.

"She came out to tease me. That made me mad. So I chased her down the sandbar. And at the end she jumped off into the water, laughing. But she never came up from her dive. That scared all of us. We thought she had drowned.

"She was never seen after that. The older people thought she moved away and were happy about it. Me and the boys knew different but we said nothing. The boys thought we might get arrested.

"At first I thought like they did. But as the years went by I figured out it was just a witch trick. She became a river spirit, that's all. Ask people on the river, there's something wrong out there. Ask them if there isn't something strange about the Winneshiek Slough. Or ask if they haven't seen odd things at night on that island off the mouth of Sugar Creek.

"She's out there. I know it. I know she is. She calls my name. That's why I don't go out on the river anymore. If I give her a chance she's going to pull me under.

"The witch is got it out for me!"

Treaty Ground Ghosts

Prairie du Chien is fertile ghost territory. The abundance of spirits is attributed to the depth of historical events at this location. Anecdotes relating to the full range of European-American occupation of the site are easily found: early French traders, British soldiers, and Mississippi boatmen.

American Indian ghosts are rarer but are commonly associated with nearby bluffs and islands. Many of these tales involve tribal chiefs of long ago, medicine men who died fighting evil, and young warriors remembered for acts of bravery.

French blood in Prairie du Chien families is the chief vehicle for preservation of these American Indian stories. Those families generally assume that their French ancestors were at least part American Indian in their bloodlines.

Several sources gave me leads on ghost stories arising from European-American and American Indian interactions. Most of these tales drew upon the hardships and brutality of war. These were fragments of older stories relating to ambushes and scalpings during the War of 1812, the Winnebago War, and the Black Hawk War.

Only one source knew of a broader context to these fragments. Surprisingly it was not a context of violent death in combat. Instead, it was in the context of diplomacy, deceit, and deception.

🌿 🌿 🌿

"They are called the Treaty Ground Ghosts," said Luke, the retired Villa Louis guide.

"They are usually seen in groups of three or four. But a dozen is not that uncommon. Even larger groups have been seen around the old Fort Crawford burial plot.

"The history of these ghosts is a little unclear. The popular version is that they started appearing after the capture and imprisonment of Black Hawk. But my family tradition has it that the sightings simply intensified at that time.

"My old St. Clair grandpapa said that the ghosts have been here for many more years than that. His Potawatomie grandmama said that Prairie du Chien has been a council and ceremonial site for many years before the white man.

"His memories of her stories were filled with references to great chiefs. Not great in the way we think of leaders today. They were great in the sense of honor and dignity and Solomon-like wisdom.

"Some of these chiefs also had status in Indian religions. Some were said to possess magical powers. Others were thought to be pure beings of half-human, half-spirit parentage.

"The Potawatomie grandmama was certain that a secret burial ground for these great ones was on the Villa Louis site. She was also certain that the graves were never found or desecrated. Nevertheless, she thought the white occupation of the site greatly disturbed their ghosts.

"But as far as pinpointing the upsurge in ghostly activity, she spoke of a different date than 1832. According to her the current ghost pattern of activity started in 1825.

"That was the year of the Prairie du Chien Treaty of 1825. It was sometimes called the Great Council of 1825. The Potawatomie grandmama called it the 'time of the great betrayal.'

"It was a turning point in Great Lakes and upper Mississippi Valley history—Territorial Governor Cass was able to summon the leadership of the Sioux, Chippewa, Ioway, Sac, Fox, Menominee, Winnebago, Ottawa, and Potawatomie tribes and got them to sign a treaty agreeing to boundary lines and tribal territories. Thousands of tribal members saw the pipe smoked and the agreement marked.

"This was the end of the Indian concept of land ownership in this area. And it is important to remember that these tribes had not been militarily defeated at this point.

"Soon there was a feeling among Indians that they had been duped. This was when the stories of the Treaty Ground Ghosts turned from benign presences into active crusaders.

"Initially, the Army garrison commander and the federal Indian agent bore the brunt of the hauntings. Faces of the old chiefs and medicine men were seen at night outside the windows of the quarters and offices of these officials.

"Between the Civil War and World War Two the visits were bestowed on local politicians, clergy, bankers, and at least one newspaper editor. Then in the 1950s the hauntings shifted back to state and federal bureaucrats.

"These ghosts became sentinels against greed and corruption. Their harassment of state and federal officials was seen as poetic justice. But their vigils outside the homes of local officials were viewed with combinations of humor and embarrassment.

"Now the current pattern is a bit different. The chief targets these days are Corps of Engineers officials and representatives of federal disaster agencies. But the ghosts are not above paying courtesy calls on the higher-up of the Wisconsin Department of Natural Resources.

"It's not a political party thing. It's not related to issues. They're brought out by whoever is peddling the biggest lies. These ghosts are better b.s. detectors than bartenders.

"I have heard from motel maids and maintenance men about the rooms of officials being turned topsy-turvy. Mechanics have told me about new government vehicles that suddenly do not work.

"Hauntings and harassment are pretty much the rule. But there are two exceptions. One when the big campout comes out here by the river. Then the ghosts are seen calmly watching by the dozens in the flickering shadows thrown by campfires.

"The other exception was a dinner held in town after the Bad Axe ceremony a few years ago. Did you know that the State apologized for the massacre? Anyway, some ministers and tribal leaders broke bread in a local supper club.

"That was the first time anyone remembers anything other than a sour look on the faces of those ghosts. Some were smiling and some had tears rolling down their cheeks.

"My guess is that our Treaty Ground Ghosts would throw one heck of a pow-wow if we could do something to clear the air about that 1825 Treaty. I can close my eyes and just imagine all those chiefs from long ago, and the ghosts of the thousands who came in 1825, gathering on the treaty grounds and finding peace at last."

The Chinese Spooks of Shanghai Ridge

Natives in the vicinity of the village of Eastman delight in spinning stories about how Shanghai Ridge came by its name.

Most of the explanations fail to ring with authenticity. Indeed, most are downright preposterous. The winner in this category has to be the assertion that Shanghai is a Norwegian corruption of "hang high."

However, these little exhibits of local color were of only passing interest until a few chance remarks revealed a related ghost story.

It is true that there is barely enough here to sketch out a tale. But any mention of Chinese ghosts in Wisconsin is unusual enough to merit inclusion in a collection.

❦   ❦   ❦

The Chinese Spooks are up on Shanghai Ridge, according to the oldtimers.

Shanghai Ridge Road cuts east from Eastman before it deadends on Haddock Hill Road. The road has a few bad turns and a rough surface here and there. It is a road that locals avoid at night.

The Chinese Spooks were first seen along the road when it was barely a mud-rutted trail. It was said that the road was more heavily traveled in those days since it bore the wagon traffic between Eastman and Steuben.

"It was in the wagon days when the Chinese Spooks were spotted," piped up one source at an Eastman gathering.

Heads nodded.

Although the presence of Asian spirits was generally deemed significant, there was a dearth of ideas about just what was significant about these spirits.

The sightings were not numerous. Perhaps once or twice a decade.

The incidents were not particularly horrifying or colorful. No angry kung fu attacks or noisy lunar New Year parades.

The descriptions all seemed to fall into the Nineteenth Century stereotype of pig-tailed coolies. That very term lead to another local confusion with the geographic feature "coulee."

Several distinct versions of the origins of these ghosts were put forth for my benefit. Fortunately these variations were less numerous and less outlandish than the explanations of the origin of Shanghai Ridge.

The variations fell into two major categories. One involved actual Chinese who died up on the ridge. The other involved the "importation" of these spirits.

"My great-great uncle—and he was older than these hills—said a gang of Chinese froze to death up there," claimed one of the Eastman benchwarmers.

Half of the group more or less agreed with this account. However, there was some dispute as to whether the Chinese were on their way to work on a railroad tunnel or if they were fleeing some evil person or force.

"No, in my family it was said a sailor brought back those ghosts in his sea trunk," insisted another.

The other half of the group was more divided on specifics. They agreed only that someone brought the ghosts.

Some were sure that a Marine brought them back in a vase he stole from a burial ground.

Others thought a merchant had brought them from Hong Kong in an ivory inlaid box.

One was positive that they were brought back by a cursed clergyman who had returned from missionary service in Canton.

Only one source confessed to actually seeing the ghosts.

"I've seen the Chinese Spooks. They're not really spooky. They're sad. They trudge along like Moses' people building the pyramids before they were free. Makes you wonder how long they have to wander up on Shanghai Ridge."

Vinegar Ridge Hunter

THE HUNTSMAN'S GHOST is a common European tale. In North America such stories are usually directly traceable to roots in England, Scotland, Germany, or Norway.

Sometimes it is possible to link a New World variant directly to specific tales carried by immigrants from such places as the Black Forest or the Inverness Wood. Other times the ghost has a clearly local genesis, with Old World elements grafted on by grandmothers and great-uncles.

Wisconsin's abundance of hunting folklore does not translate into many ghost stories with a purely hunting context. Perhaps hunting is such a large part of life in rural Wisconsin that it is devoid of the mystery necessary to generate a ghost tale.

Yet such tales do exist (one right on my farm in Iowa County). However they usually deal with rather benign spirits of conventional habits.

Crawford County's contribution to this tradition stands apart from the usual Wisconsin tales about ghosts of hunters whose love of the woods kept them afield in the afterlife.

The Vinegar Ridge Hunter is unusual in many respects. He dates back to Crawford County's earliest days. He is a competitive, even aggressive, spirit (with a hint of Winny Beaujeau). He evokes strong feelings.

"For years I was sure that the Vinegar Ridge Hunter was an undercover conservation warden," spat Don, the Petersburg "outdoorsman."

"I fancy myself to be like the old time woodsmen. Not a sportsman, mind you. No way. Every deer I pick off or pick up, every ice chest full of panfish, is one less day fixing somebody's roof or painting their barn.

"So I find my independence outdoors. That's why I don't take kindly to this Vinegar Ridge Hunter even if the S.O.B. isn't a warden.

"Anyone who messes with a man's living is lower than a scum-sucking dog. Especially around here, where, if you haven't noticed, we ain't got pots to plop in. I mean, recovery or recession—shoot, you can't even tell which in Crawford County.

"I heard these ghost stories since I was a boy. But for years I thought the stories were just excuses made by a bunch of sorry cross-eyed dipsticks who couldn't find a deer if it mounted them from behind.

"But I finally learned different the hard way. That's when I made it my business to learn everything I could about him.

"So I had to talk to all sorts of old drooling geezers. Shoot, half of them can't even keep their pants dry. I told my old lady to use the .44 on me if I end up that way.

"I learned that the story goes right back to territory days. The old farts all agree that the Vinegar Ridge Hunter was a veteran of the Black Hawk War.

"Not your run-of-the-mill plow jockey or boozing lead miner. And not your lace kerchief federal officer.

"No he was a Swiss-born professional soldier who had served in the French Army. He did time in wars in Europe, Asia, and Africa and hunted in all those places. He grew up sturdy in the Alps.

"He cashed out of that military business and came to America to seek his fortune. Came up the Mississippi and hooked up with the rough Missouri crowd. You know those thugs Colonel Dodge brought up to run off Indians and claim-jump on land and mines.

"After that point the old geezers start to disagree. Some say that those Missouri bushwhackers killed him. A few even think that the Missouri boys turned him into beef jerky and sold him over at Ft. Crawford.

"Others say that a panther got him. That was supposed to be the end result of a curse by an African witch doctor.

"I guess it doesn't really matter what happened. But it does figure in on why the ghost does what he does.

"I don't really know why he's linked to Vinegar Ridge. It's true that many sightings are west of Mount Zion mostly in the towns of Haney and Scott. Right along Highway W often as not.

"But I've heard of sightings in Crow Hollow and Childs Hollow, too. So there is some range.

"Some say the actual identity is lost. Others say it was covered up to protect descendants. And one old bonebag was one hundred percent sure that there was a connection to the Steiner family.

"There's also disagreement about what the Vinegar Ridge Hunter does when he shows up. Some have him wearing a sword and trotting around on horseback behind a pack of hounds. Others, and I'm in this bunch, experience weird deals where a man is there one minute and an animal is there the next.

"The Indians call this shape-shifting. I read up on it. It's in a lot of their old hunting stories.

"But no matter how you cut it he's an annoying, maybe even dangerous, ghost. He's always screwing up hunting for people. He's caused accidents. He might be the cause of some of the shootings we've had over the years.

"He's startled people and made them slip off cliffs. He's pushed people out of tree stands. He's plugged up and blown up shotgun barrels.

"And I know of some things he's done other than bother hunters. He's likely to show up anytime you need some privacy.

"My last encounter with the darn so-and-so was when I was doing a little woodcutting. There are these Chicago ding-a-lings who have some land up here. A storm blew down some of their trees. So I knew they couldn't miss those four big walnuts. They meant a whole month off for me.

"Anyway, I was just about done. I was chaining down the logs. Darn, if my chainsaw doesn't start itself up and come chasing after me.

"That brings me back to why he does what he does.

"The one way of thinking has it that he's a protector of animals. Heck, the whole environment.

"That comes out of his killing animals all over the world, the witch doctor curse, and his being eaten by the panther. He's setting right what he did before.

"The other way of thinking has it that his murder by the bush-whackers turned him into a ghostly Lone Ranger or Dirty Harry. You know, a do-gooder and busybody.

"Now this would be okay if he focused on the big stuff. But you'd think a powerful ghost would have better stuff to do than worry about me popping four turkeys or keeping those trout from the catch-and-release area.

"It's not like he's breaking up the Colombian gangs or stopping wars. Cripes, it's just penny ante-stuff out here.

"I've seen him operate on others. There's these two Indians who come over from the Dells. They shoot deer for some kind of ceremony feasts. They can't wait on the season for that.

"What's the harm? It's only three or four deer a year.

"Anyhow, the ghost chased them out of the woods. Chased them right into their big old Pontiac. They threw it in reverse and backed into a ditch just as the warden came by. So they lost their guns and got a big fine, too.

"Then another time I saw two old boys road-hunting. It looked like they were getting set up with the DNR decoy. You know, that stuffed deer they use to entrap people.

"Well these guys didn't even get off a shot. The decoy came to life and chased them down the road. Then they cracked up.

"I just don't get it. He's often seen fox and coon hunting. So does he want to keep all the game to himself? Or does he just stick to his own personal code?

"I know I'm tired of it. I'm thinking of moving up north where the living and the dead don't pester you so much!"

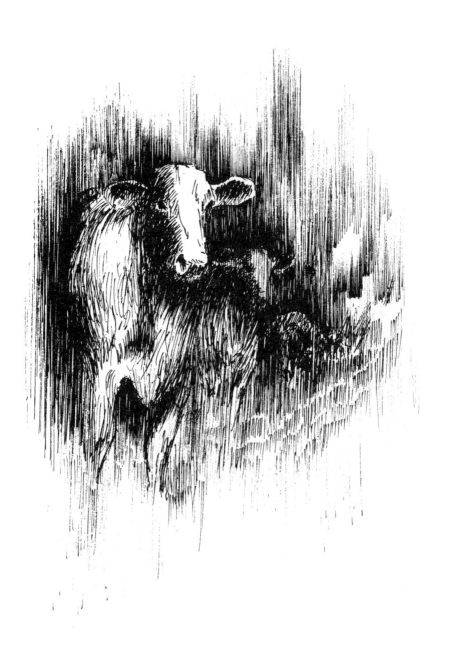

Part Four

Sauk County

Lime Ridge's Cows

ANIMAL GHOSTS MAKE their presence felt in many areas of Wisconsin. Ghosts of big game animals are often seen in the northern part of the state. Dog, coyote, and wolf ghosts occupy specific niches in Wisconsin lore. Even ghosts of prehistoric and extinct beasts find their way into local legends.

Wisconsin being the dairy state, it should probably come as no surprise that we also boast one bovine-related ghost story. One might suspect that such a story would center on some beloved "Bossy" tragically burned in a barn fire or some prized purebred murdered by cutthroat competitors.

Instead we find at Lime Ridge an entire herd of mysterious origin.

🌿 🌿 🌿

The Lime Ridge Cows seem to be of recent vintage. No one recalls hearing of them before Nineteen Fifty Seven. Bits and pieces of the story can be heard from Hill Point to Ironton. But the focus is generally Lime Ridge.

Oddly enough it is hard to find anyone in the Lime Ridge neighborhood who can report much more than hearsay. To secure details it is necessary to scour the feedmills of Plain and Loganville and the cheese factories of Carr Valley and Cedar Grove.

Even a pile of details does not a ghost story make. If often takes an interpreter to make sense of random finds. A stop in Loganville in search of fabled raspberry pie produced an interpreter in the form of a coffee-sipping cafe regular.

Almost every truck stop and greasy spoon has someone who fills this slot. They nurse cups of lukewarm java for hours. They provide running commentary on community affairs. They afford less humor than town drunks but are often accorded far more dignity.

But they are rarely good sources for ghosts stories. In their world of informal coffee talk, reference to spirits falls in with the impolite topics of sex, politics, and religion.

Our Loganville coffee drinker was an exception. He clearly felt the need to be a booster of all northwestern Sauk County has to offer, from Amish quilts to hidden fishing holes.

"Some say the Lime Ridge Cows are a dairy heretic's story," he laughed. "That's because the whole herd is Brown Swiss. You can imagine how that drives these Holstein fanatics crazy.

"Now there are old fellows who claim that the cow ghosts are kind of a protest against Holsteins. I don't think I'd go that far. But it could be that those cow ghosts do stand as a reminder of a certain way of life. Before everything got big and the corporations ran it all.

"You know, most people don't even remember anything other than black-and-white cows. We forgot that dozens and dozens of different breeds of livestock, pigs, sheep, horses, and poultry made the countryside a colorful place. Made for safer genetics. Not all the eggs in one basket as it were.

"The Lime Ridge Cows are from a special time in Wisconsin. It's a herd of about two dozen. That's the size most farmers had in the forties and fifties. Those were the days when you could milk and make a living without a lot of machinery or debt. So these particular cows are a symbol of something we've lost.

"No one knows whose herd it was or if it is a group that came together from different places. They often walk single file along the roads at night. Don't think that doesn't throw off some drivers.

"The drunks are lucky. They just drive through the cow ghosts and just blink their eyes. The sober drivers often swerve and damage their cars. One old fellow tried to put their wanderings to an end. He tried to lead them to an abandoned barn in the area. But the cows balked at the door.

"My theory is that those cows are waiting for things to get straightened out. When we get back to a country life that works, then those cows will go home."

Whiskey Jack

TALL TALES STEMMING from larger-than-life characters are common along the whole length of the Wisconsin River.

Such stories are at least in part based on the exploits of real-life local heroes whose reputations grew through years of storytelling embellishment.

Whiskey Jack is different from those other characters in that the stories of his ghost's exploits are as treasured as the tales of his life-time heroics.

Both his earthly and his ghostly accomplishments have a decidedly Nineteenth Century flavor. Almost all the stories have logging or lumber themes.

Whiskey Jack was a local boy who made good up in the northern pinewoods lumber camps. He was a local version of Paul Bunyan. He stood seven-foot three-inches and weighed 310 pounds.

Stories of his lifetime accomplishments focus on youthful deeds in Medford, Prentice, and Phillips. By his middle years—after the pine forest clearcutting—we find a few tales of Whiskey Jack working the lower Wisconsin River.

He was a more mellow hero by then. He was lifting stray cows back over fences instead of fighting dozens of lumberjacks singlehandedly or wrestling bears. In those years he had his own crew of "log miners" who "reaped" logs called "volunteer timber." This business consisted of pulling unclaimed logs out of the muck of sandbars, sloughs, and side creeks.

In this period of his life he was connected to the various larger-than-life characters of southwest Wisconsin: River Rat Fred, the Wyalusing Snake Man, Phineas Flintlock, Iron Lena, and a cousin, Apple Jack. There are also whole collections of little stories about Whiskey Jack and his interactions with these other characters which are simply jokes on the order of the Catholic, the Protestant, and the Jew in a rowboat, or the priest, the banker, and the lawyer on a deserted island.

Perhaps the best known tale of his river work has to do with how he met his death. This final act of heroism is honored more than his other achievements because it was an incredible rescue of two children.

The two kids (one a Mickelson boy and the other a Kane) were playing out on a big logjam on the river early one spring. The thaw was loosening things up and Whiskey Jack was trying to open a jam in order to pull the logs he wanted into a nearby slough. He did not see the kids until after the jam started to move.

By the time he spotted them the jam gave a big crack and logs were riding a crest of foamy water. The kids were clinging to branches as the big tree they rode on alternately submerged and rocketed out of the water.

Whiskey Jack made a mad dash across this tidal wave of logs. He jumped from log to log like a kangaroo. He pushed massive stray logs out of his way with his sharp peavey. Logs were splintering and exploding.

He reached the boys just as their tree rolled over and the main part of the jam was about to pass over them. He dove under the crunching logs and came up with them both.

He flung the Mickelson boy, then threw the Kane boy all the way to shore. The boys later said it was like being shot out of a cannon.

Whiskey Jack was then pulled under the mass of grinding logs and debris.

This was supposed to have happened near Grape Island where the county lines of Dane, Iowa, and Sauk meet in the Wisconsin River.

Whiskey Jack's body didn't show up for a week. When it did, he conveniently washed up on the shore of Long Island, near Lone Rock.

That is where the ghost story begins.

🔥 🔥 🔥

"They said he looked like a bloated dead ox," Mike, the Spring Green farmer related matter-of-factly.

"Whiskey Jack was lucky in some ways, though. He could have been eel chow. Instead he came up right where he had some friends.

"Now they were weird friends, that's true. On Long Island in those days you had moonshiners and fugitives living out there. And the big rascal River Rat Fred.

"Old Fred is responsible for the whole mess. He got Whiskey Jack's soul so it just couldn't rest.

"Don't get me wrong. They were friends. They just thought differently. Whiskey Jack was a simple soul. River Rat Fred was a character given to ivory canes and top hats.

"Old Fred took over the funeral and turned it into a spectacle. First off the mangled and waterlogged body shouldn't have been displayed at a funeral. Whiskey Jack looked like a mildewed mound of lard.

"Then there was the coffin. A regular one wouldn't do. So old Fred found a piano crate and had it lined with silk and painted up with French bordello pictures.

"The final insult was the clothing. Whiskey Jack was definitely an overalls man. But old Fred had a tailor make a Louie the Fourteenth suit with lace cuffs.

"They then buried him on the eastern point of Long Island in a big blow-out drunk that lasted two days. Whiskey Jack would have liked that part. But his soul was unsettled and it wasn't long before his ghost made its first appearance. A week after the burial his spirit popped up out the river and threw old Fred off a boat.

"It was the first of many such encounters between the two. Sometimes Whiskey Jack's ghost would fling old Fred's boats clear out of the water.

"Whiskey Jack kept up this harassment for as long as River Rat Fred was around here. You know, of course, that old Fred disappeared at sea.

"That left Whiskey Jack without his main target for revenge. Now it would have been better if they could have been ghost buddies on the Wisconsin River. Instead old Fred is in a clipper ship somewhere at the bottom of the Pacific.

"So Whiskey Jack changed his routine. He found a new mission in helping people on the river and loggers in the woods. I've heard many tales about his rescues. I can't say if half of them are true. But I saw something that proves it to me. It involved my nephew. We were fishing out of my boat close to the Highway 23 bridge.

"The boy fell out of the boat when we bumped a log. I shouldn't been out so late. He got away quick on the current. He yelled but I couldn't see him. I was probably more scared than he was. But I thought for sure I lost him. Then on the island near the bridge I heard coughing. I moved in close and there was a big man pulling the boy out of the water. The big fellow just gently laid the boy on the sand and headed into the brush. I yelled to him but he didn't even look back.

"My nephew claims that he sank into one of those twenty foot holes. He just assumed he was a goner. Then someone grabbed him. My nephew said that his rescuer was the biggest man he ever saw. A hand that could encircle the boy's thigh.

"The boy said that the big fellow told him to be more cautious: 'Be careful or else you'll live in the river with me,' said the big man."

Rocky Arbor Battle Ghosts

MANY OF THE stories in this collection graphically make the point that ghost stories are intimately connected to broader folklore currents.

It is a barren ghost story which draws nothing from local tradition, personalities, and ethnic culture. Overlap of a ghost story with a folktale is the rule rather than the exception.

Here we find a ghost story that stands on its own, and that is also connected to several distinct folklore traditions. The connections are made even more unusual by virtue of the time frames of the three folklore traditions: ancient, pioneer, and contemporary.

It is the ancient tale that provides the basic framework for the ghost story. The Rocky Arbor Battle Ghosts draw directly from the legend of Red Horn.

Red Horn connects the oral traditions of the Ho Chunk people with southwest Wisconsin's most incredible cave art.

The stories and the ancient paintings tell the story of a battle thought to have been fought between the area's original inhabitants and Viking interlopers. This bloody battle caused many casualties that in turn pursued ghostly combat in the afterlife.

I have assigned this story to Sauk County because of its Rocky Arbor location and because I first overheard reference to it at a Sauk City dairy

bar. But in all fairness it must be conceded that the sightings range from
Roche A Cri to Wisconsin Heights.

The wide geographical span of sightings is consistent with the legend
of a running battle through the central Wisconsin River valley over several days, with the final stand and destruction of the Vikings coming in
the area just south of Rocky Arbor State Park.

A large, extended Sauk County family cultivates these tales. Red
beards, blond curls, and northern European surnames hide their partial
Ho Chunk blood.

The chief guardian of the stories is a middle-aged blond woman who
lovingly tends gardens, trees, and greenhouses as well as stories. She
speaks with equal warmth of Winnebago cousins and visits to distant
relatives in Norway. It is her habit to take her morning coffee in Sauk
City and agitate the older regulars with her broadminded views of life.

Let's eavesdrop.

🌾 🌾 🌾

"You hear more about the Red Horn legend now that the Iowa
County rock art has been interpreted," Donna beamed.

"I've been telling that story to people for years and they thought I
was half-crazy. Well, they probably thought I was totally crazy. But now
I have a little credibility, so I'm going to remind everyone who told
them first.

"Most of what I know comes from my cousin Marjorie. Actually, she's
a second cousin and almost twenty years older than me.

"She lived a traditional Winnebago life over by an isolated shack near
Natural Bridge. She spent summers gathering berries and herbs. And I
spent a summer with her when I was a girl.

"Marjorie was just fulled to the brim with lore and wisdom. She
talked constantly about eating the right diet and taking care of the body.
She talked about the parallels between the sweat lodge and the sauna.
And she was a walking history of odd interactions between Winnebagos
and Norwegians.

"Before I go further I should mention that I do not approve of non-
Indians borrowing or hybridizing Indian stories. Do not take what does
not belong to you! But I see these tales as an exception because this is

really all about how the stories were interpreted by Norwegian-Winne-bago-Americans. How's that for hyphens?

"Marjorie would talk openly about the Red Horn ghosts at Rocky Arbor because she saw them differently than other people.

"Those invested in continued racial friction saw the ghosts as locked in eternal combat. Marjorie saw them as now reconciled warriors who playfully practiced fighting.

"Her angle has everything going for it. For in the hundreds of years of ghost fighting no one has reported ghostly gore. It's always clashing clubs and axes and loud whoops.

"And it's Marjorie's angle which helps make sense of the so-called 'Battle of Four Corners' which took place just to the east of the Rocky Arbor area. As you know, this is the local tale about the time when the federal government was going to push the Winnebago out of Wisconsin. And it is true that a a bunch of Norwegian and German pioneers took their guns and ran the government men off.

"But the so-called battle would be hard to explain if it didn't dove-tail with the Rocky Arbor Red Horn ghosts. Marjorie said that a Menomonie scout with the government men told the story that a com-bination of Indians and giant white men with red beards ran out of the woods at night into the government camp. Apparently the government men didn't stop running until they got to Green Bay.

"So in Marjorie's view those Norwegian and German settlers could not take the full credit for the rescue of the Winnebago.

"She also tied the Red Horn Rocky Arbor ghosts into the Battle of Wisconsin Heights. In the historical accounts there is the mystery of 'the voice' in the dark which so scared the soldiers. Marjorie was certain that Red Horn was 'the voice' and that a contingent of Winnebago and Viking ghosts was the real rearguard at Wisconsin Heights when Black Hawk and the Sauk slipped across the river.

"Marjorie said that Black Hawk made a habit of conjuring up spir-its and such wherever he went. He had shamans and sorcerers to guide him. He even had a habit of fighting battles near mounds where he could draw on their power. When he lost in the end it was because he was cut off from his usual sources.

"Marjorie also referred to something else about Red Horn that I didn't understand. She said that he worked with 'the trickster' and that explained what happened at Four Corners and at Wisconsin Heights and what has happened more recently.

"Frankly, this trickster was always mumble-jumbo to me. At first I thought that she meant a shaman or medicine man. But later I figured out that it was something more like a powerful spirit, kind of a devil with a sense of humor.

"Marjorie did point out two times when Red Horn's ghosts and the trickster intervened in modern-day events.

"She said in 1989 a bunch of local yahoos invited the anti-treaty grand dragons down to speak at a Lake Delton event. She and a couple of other traditionalists went to stand outside the hall and keep an eye on things.

"She saw the ghosts right in the parking lot that night and saw the trickster on the roof of the meeting hall. Funny thing was, that meeting did break up under unusual circumstances, with people hotfooting out of the hall and racing down the road in the pickups.

"Then more recently she said the ghosts and the trickster had a run-in with those 'concerned landowner' pinheads along the river. You know, the ones who think that the Lower Wisconsin Riverway is some plot of the United Nations, the New World Order, Jewish Bankers in Switzerland, and the Tri-lateral Commission.

"Well apparently these conspiracy fanatics had their undies in a bundle over the Winnebago buying land down near Muscoda. Somehow their feeble minds tied this land purchase into a big bundle of socialism, casino corruption, and DNR oppression.

"So they called a big meeting over in Plain. I guess all of eight people showed up. But Marjorie and two friends did their usual vigil and they saw the ghosts there. And I guess the trickster flattened the tires on eight pickups that night.

"There was a quilt that had the embroidered story of Red Horn, Rocky Arbor, Four Corners, and the trickster in pictures. A distant part of the family over by Merrimac had it. It was sold in an estate sale. I couldn't believe they sold it without telling anybody else in the family.

"People always ask me where they can see the ghosts. As if they're on the chamber of commerce tour brochure.

"Ghosts decide when you can see them. And these particular ghosts seem to let themselves be seen along the Upper Dells mostly at dawn. They're seen by boaters at the south end of Black Hawk Island.

"I've heard of sightings of them in canoes on Mirror Lake. I've heard of them dancing around a big fire up on the Baraboo Bluffs. I've even heard they sat down to a feast with some real live people. But I'm not saying who or where."

Reedburg's Rag Lady

IT IS OFTEN difficult to tell where a ghost story ends and the broader folklore context begins.

Usually it is the ghost story that has the greater notoriety. Any underlying folktales or folklore context typically require a bit of digging to unearth them.

On occasion a folktale will yield an auxiliary ghost story when a bashful source finally overcomes his or her embarrassment over talking about ghosts.

Perhaps it is partly a matter of sources telling investigators what the sources think the investigators want to hear.

But it is the collector of stories who must concede embarrassment when the folktale and the ghost story are well in hand and the light bulb of connection finally goes on.

The embarrassment is further compounded when the collector must revisit the sources of both strands of the common tale and hear the common refrain: "Well, you didn't ask about that other part."

This story is a concession of such embarrassment on my part.

🌿 🌿 🌿

The folktale of the Rag Lady was a bit of a riddle in and of itself. Of a half dozen sources, all but one spoke of a "ragman."

It was a real treat to uncover the gender mystery of a grandmother hidden under baggy clothes and a floppy hat.

The folktale had many charming elements. A kindly older person driving a horse-drawn junk wagon. Little gifts for children and food and clothing for the poor.

The ghost story had many of the same elements. Presents out of the blue and mysterious good deeds.

The Rag Lady as a folktale was focused in and around Reedsburg but did involve much of northern Sauk County and parts of adjoining counties.

The ghost story is far more localized. The Rag Lady's wagon is seen only on Old Ironton Road and Schutte Road. Wagon sightings are not common. Once or twice a year seems to be the norm.

The wagon is sighted just before dawn. All the sightings are clustered in late May and early June. A mountain of carpets, egg crates, and bundles of rags are seen in a swaying pile atop the wagon. The driver is hidden in baggy overalls with her face shadowed by a broad brim hat.

"I've only seen the wagon once," conceded a Town of Ironton farmer. "But when I saw it I was certainly surprised. I was in a hurry that morning.

"It had just rained and the road was slick on the way to Reedsburg. After I crossed Silver Creek I came to that big curve in the woods. I'll admit I took the curve too far on the inside—the wrong side of the road. Well I almost hit the wagon. I swerved and went into a skid, said a few choice words, and continued on my way.

"But I hadn't gone far before it sank in about what had happened. I mean I've had close calls with horse-drawn vehicles before. But it occurred to me that this wasn't an Amish vehicle and it wasn't a gaudy parade wagon pulled by a show team.

"The Rag Lady story came to mind. My Grandfather had seen the same thing fifty years before. So I turned the truck around.

"But when I got back to the curve—no horses, no wagon, and no Rag Lady. No tracks on the shoulder. No horse apples. So where did she go?"

The other aspect of the Rag Lady ghost is a bit more subtle. There are no sightings associated with the Rag Lady's Reedsburg visits.

In a few of the oldest sections of Reedsburg the Rag Lady is still said to leave small gifts on back porches. It is also clear that such incidents are clearly on the decline. During the Great Depression the gifts were very common.

During the Rag Lady's life she is said to have helped widows to avoid mortgage foreclosure by walking into banks and paying off loans. She also helped other women start up businesses. But those good deeds are now four generations removed from common conversation.

After the Rag Lady's death, gifts still found their way to the homes of the less fortunate. "The old people said it started with hand-sewn clothing for children," asserted Emma, the retired school secretary.

"Later we heard of handmade dolls for poor children. And chicken soup for sick shut-ins. And pies for old bachelors.

"There was a row of little houses south of the railroad track. I think they're all gone now. That's where many of these gifts showed up.

"Over the years you heard less and less about it. But we'd still hear of a jar of homemade jam here and there. Now and then someone will still talk about a pot of noodles left on the back porch. Sometimes it's simply a gift from a friendly neighbor.

"But if the secret delivery comes early—before breakfast—and if there is the tinkling of the old junk wagon bell. Well, then it's really the Rag Lady."

Part Five

Lafayette County

The School House Specter

LAFAYETTE COUNTY HAS a rich tradition of rural schools. There is even a folklore claim to the first school in Wisconsin. That claim rests on definitional criteria of education conducted in a building erected for that purpose for at least two years (thus disqualifying the church and store schools operating for intermittent one-year periods in Iowa and Grant counties).

That first school was supposedly located between Benton and Strawbridge. No physical evidence remains.

Such is the fate of many Lafayette County rural schools. One could make the case that more rural schools have vanished in Lafayette County than in any other Wisconsin county.

In large part this is due to the early origins of those schools. Most were rough pioneer structures. There are tales of sod roof dugouts and stick-and-clay huts being used for schools. Needless to say, most of these structures did not make it into the Twentieth Century.

What did survive was a vast store of schoolhouse folklore, including ghost stories. There are literally hundreds of tales concerning teachers, school outhouses, schoolyard pranks and fights, scholarly achievements, and embarrassing dunces. And there are dozens of schoolhouse ghosts.

Or are there?

The question must be raised because the source for this story suggests that one ghost serves a number of school locations.

🔥 🔥 🔥

"I have personally heard of school ghosts in eleven old Lafayette County schools," states Dorothy, the retired teacher, with precision. She rattles off the forgotten names and locations of one-room schools in the towns of Wiota, Wayne, Argyle, Fayette, Willow Springs, Belmont, Elk Grove, Seymour, Gratiot, Monticello, and White Oak Springs.

As she talks, she flits around her tidy Blanchardville apartment, fussing over school memorabilia. Class photos line the walls and shelves and end tables bear heavy loads of school bells, ink wells, and old books.

Our storyteller here taught in one-room schools from 1937 to 1946. She came up through the old normal school system of teacher education. During that time she taught in five schools: three in Lafayette County, one in Green County, and one in Iowa County. Her teaching career started as a way of helping her family keep their farm during the Depression. Then World War Two's labor shortages made her feel needed until the country felt normal again.

She is reluctant to tackle the ghost story directly. Like many sources she is concerned that she establish her credibility first. She goes to great lengths to demonstrate the clarity of her memory and the sharpness of all her senses.

Finally she could no long avoid the topic at hand. "You will pardon my prattling," she apologized.

"The school in question is the red brick building with the bell tower on Highway 78. It is on that road as you go south from Blanchardville, south of Kainz Road. Or north from Argyle north of Sawmill Road.

"It is a distinctive school building. Something about the brick. It's not as old as many schools are. The site is odd, too. Sitting on the hillside as it does.

"It was a pretty site at one time. I remember lilacs and a line of daffodils. There is still a nice grove of black and bur oak there. But at one time there were a few sugar maples, a catalpa, and a buckeye.

"I must admit it is a bit shabby there now. The weeds are high, the flagpole is rusty, and the old pump has tumbled down.

"But it is a fitting home for a ghost. Or perhaps its second or third home at this site. For it is said that at least one frame school preceded the brick and that perhaps a log school preceded the frame school. On top of those allegations there is the claim that an early pioneer church was on or near this site and that school was held in it for a time.

"Now the ghost is a curious matter. No one can discern a pattern of his appearances. He might be seen nightly for a week and then disappear for months.

"That leads to the theory, which I heard years ago and have come to believe, that this school ghost may be present at some or all of the other haunted school sites I mentioned. And perhaps he is active at some other old schools as well.

"The thought behind this theory is the old custom of the itinerant school teacher.

"There was a time when teachers were in very short supply. Back in the time when teachers were almost exclusively men, they would often teach a year at one rural school. Then they would seek a better deal down the road. They often negotiated for a bit more money, but often it was a matter of better room and board. Or sometimes a milk cow, chickens, and a garden plot to use.

"The old farmers tried to get by as cheap as possible. You could say the complaints about school costs were already fairly sharp in those days. This made it easy for the village down the road with the doctor, the pastor, and the tavern to steal away the rural school's teacher. Especially if the doctor, pastor, and the tavernkeeper had eligible daughters.

"I won't go into all of the problems of male teacher courting and breach of promise. But let me say that rural education did not stabilize until women took over.

"At the school in question, here, the ghost has his routine. He starts in the early morning, about 4 a.m., with lighting of kerosene lamps. You can see the glow through the dirty windows. Then you can see smoke rise out of the chimney as he starts a fire to warm the school. Next the squeaky pump creaks when he fills the water bucket.

"All this usually occurs without seeing him. Although a few people claim to see a shadow.

"The creaking pump is usually the end of it. But a few people have heard old-time Christmas carols played on the old upright piano. One or two have seen the kerosene lamps burn late into the evening.

"At the other school the routine is very similar. That is what makes us think it is the same ghost.

"The ghosts or the ghost appearances at Willow Springs and White Oak Springs are concluded at days end by the clopping of a horse and buggy. At Elk Grove and Gratiot the ghosts run off young trespassers with frightful noises.

"I should also mention that these incidents are not all in schools. In some cases the lights and such are seen at places where only the foundation of the school remains. In another case the school building was moved and the ghost came along.

"There are also many theories about the identity of the ghost. Some are just plain silly. For instance, the idea that the ghost was a teacher killed in the Black Hawk War. There is absolutely no basis for that claim.

"But two stories do have at least a foundation in reality. There was at least one area teacher who was killed in a buggy accident. There was also a young teacher who only taught a year or two in the area before being killed in World War One.

"I tend to believe the second story for two reasons. First, I heard the piano play a medley of tunes such as 'Over There,' 'Tipperary,' and French cafe songs. Second, there have been times when a forty-eight star flag flew at the school on Armistice Day.

"I have talked to the families out there. The Hermansons, the Fryes, the Larsons, the Moens, the Hendricksons, and others. Many have seen or heard strange things there.

"I do not know if I really believe in hauntings. Ghosts could have other explanations. But I do know that when I summoned up enough courage to go into the school I definitely felt a presence.

"The feeling itself was familiar. After a time I came to recognize why. It was the feeling I often had as a young teacher when I worked late. A feeling that all the teachers that came before you are still there to watch over and guide you."

Spirit of the Bloody Lake Rendezvous

Wisconsin's "buckskinners" and other frontier reenactment hobbyists have many standard tales that are told around rendezvous and encampment cooking fires. Many of these tales are "generic" and are swapped at such events from Kentucky to Montana.

The annual Bloody Lake Rendezvous has a rich tradition of local stories. A number of participants have honed a sharp edge on stories clearly drawn from local history and folklore.

Naturally such an environment might spawn a ghost tale or two. In this case it's a patron or mascot ghost that has joined participants at the event for more than a dozen years.

Join the group at the campfire at dusk at the Black Hawk Memorial Park near Woodford. Let the pipe smoke mix with the smells of coffee, grease drippings, and burning oak. Be patient while the tired women sigh and the men groan while holding their full bellies.

Eventually, squirming children and a growing chorus of whispers will prompt a rotund fellow in a kilt to ask if anybody has seen anything unusual.

🔥 🔥 🔥

No one has seen him so far this year. Ya know lads, the spirit, the spirit of this rendezvous. Ya canna see him every year ya come. I've seen him but thrice in ten years.

But every year some lass or laddie sees our beloved Spirit of the Bloody Lake Rendezvous. Two years ago nearly a hundred people saw the poor soul. But some years he might be observed only by a solitary pair courting in the woods beyond the tents.

You young ones might find reason to fear the apparition of this long deceased pioneer. But he canna and willna hurt you. He is a gentle if tortured soul whose years of loneliness make him seek out our companionship.

He canna enter the farms and villages. He is limited to the things of his day. Only camps like ours were around in his time.

His day, if you didna know, was of course the terrible year of 1832. It was the year of the Lord Chief Black Hawk and his Sac clan on the march through these wilds.

Our Spirit friend was caught up in the turmoil and couldna avoid militia service back in that time. Misfortune is common during war and our friend had a generous portion of bad luck. His luck turned sour from the time he joined the local militia assembling at Fort Hamilton.

Fort Hamilton was later to become Hamilton Diggings and later still Wiota, if you didna know.

Our Spirit friend couldna possibly have known that his days were numbered. After all, many thousands of volunteers mustered for the

Black Hawk War and most didna hear a single shot fired in anger. Straight off, lots were drawn for the duty of scouting and patrol. Our friend drew this assignment whilst most of his comrades were occupied with the improvement of the Fort Hamilton fortifications.

He came to lead a small band engaged in these reconnoiters and observations. He couldna done worse in the drawing of this compliment of men. That is if men they could be called under a call to arms. Old men and boys. Hardly a fit mount among them. And little in the way of powder and ball. Girded with but rusty sabers from wars past.

Our Spirit friend led several scouting parties that didna see hide nor feather of the Sac clan. But upon one fateful day he was ordered to scout toward Spafford Creek. It was an area he knew well and he didna believe the Indians would come this way.

'Tis true that Black Hawk did lead his band further east. But the old Lord canna be thought foolish. His wiles conceived a plan to send groups of his clansmen throughout the territory to sow terror and confusion.

It happened that one such group was journeying forth to Spafford Creek on a swing toward Fort Hamilton. Along came a silent raiding party under the leadership of a battle leader by the name of Little Priest.

Little Priest caught the militia men unawares. The frontiersman didn't get off so much as a single shot. The youngest of the scouts did get away and flee toward Hamilton Diggings. Our friend made his stand with his comrades.

Lads, it was hardly a fight what with strong young Sac up against elderly traders and crippled miners. There was but one bead of sweat upon Little Priest's brow before the frontiersmen were tied and staked to the ground.

Though we in this calm day canna imagine the foul things that can befall a prisoner, it must be said that even by the harsh standards of war there were such sights and sounds as to chill bone and soul.

One by one Little Priest took his evil pleasure upon the prisoners. Screams echoed through the valley.

Our friend was tormented by his role as final witness for his comrades' agonies. It was only through one surge of anger and blood that he broke his bonds and slipped away. Then like a blinded animal he ran through the wilds. He was now but a raving madman.

He raged through prairie hills and wooded glens for two days and two nights. Finally he stumbled into a Fort Hamilton alive with the celebration of the militia victory at the Battle of the Pecatonica.

The tale gets a little murky at this point. Did our friend's madness bring him to take his life by his own hand? Did a wild charge of desertion lead to a lynching?

The mists of time leave questions that canna be answered. But in these mysteries lie the origins of the transformation of a militiaman to a tormented spirit.

But fear him not in his pained wanderings. He is but a kindred spirit to we humble people gathered in our tents and lodges.

Wherever honest folks gather in camps in these valleys, you will find the Spirit of the Bloody Lake Rendezvous.

You mayna always see him. He may be but a wee presence—a wisp on the wind. But he's always there. Seeking the warmth of our company and craving a hot cup of coffee.

So remember our rules of hospitality. Make room for him by the fire and leave your lodge flaps open.

A Ghostly Glossary

GHOST STORY SOURCES rarely trouble themselves about distinctions between various spirit types.

Some stories in this collection use various terms and designation. Except for the ones with American Indian origins, there is scant examination of the basis of ghostly variations.

Relatively late in collecting these stories, I stumbled upon a Lafayette County source who puts great store in differentiation among various ghost types. This retired agricultural equipment assembler is a forty-year resident of the Strawbridge area who was born in New Diggings on the eve of the Great Depression.

His four decades of carpooling to a Dubuque factory gave him ample opportunity to swap stories and develop a broad regional appreciation of strange tales. Town of Benton friends consider him a treasure of Mississippi Valley lore and ghost tales in Jo Daviess County, Illinois, and in Iowa from Dubuque down to the Missouri state line.

He is no slouch when it comes to Lafayette and Grant counties in Wisconsin. He smoothly rattles off the various ghostly inhabitants in those two southwestern counties. In doing so he shows a sophistication about ghost types unusual for someone who does not dabble in the occult.

🌿 🌿 🌿

"Ghost types?", Sam brightens, "We have them by the dozens."

Our Strawbridge source follows with a lengthy explanation of how there are many names for ghosts and many types of ghosts. In a nutshell, there are many names that signify types but also some different names for the same types.

"It took me years to figure this out. I was hearing dozens of stories and I could sense some patterns. That got me reading some old books on the subject. I soon learned that geography, ethnic traditions, and historical events all played a role shaping these types. Just about every town has its ghosts.

"First there is your standard ghost. I call it your haunted house ghost. By that I mean one identified with a specific site.

"Now, I've heard such ghosts called 'haints,' 'spooks,' and 'bogers.' Some would say goblins, too, but I find them a bit more mobile and malicious, too.

"These haunted-house ghosts are also found in churches, taverns, schools, and cemeteries and so forth.

"There's a Benton bridge ghost, an Elk Grove house ghost, a Belmont cemetery ghost, a grain elevator ghost in Darlington, and church ghosts in Shullsburg, South Wayne, and Blanchardville. And dozens of pioneer site ghosts in Wiota, Woodford, Gratiot, Calamine, Jenkynsville and other such places.

"Those are your most common ghosts.

"Then you have your more specialized spirits. Mainly ones that haunt individuals, families, or groups with some odd event in common. These are your phantoms, specters, and manes. They are persistent, far-traveling, and often vengeful. Usually there is a hint of murder or other evil-doing here. You might call this your headless horseman type.

"We have ones like this associated with Fort Hamilton, Spafford Creek, Lead Mine, and Little Mound. In Grant County they have such things at British Hollow, Potosi, and Dickeyville.

"These stories usually have an element of pursuit and terror. Often they are linked to the disappearance of their victim. But I haven't been able to positively link a phantom chase to a proven disappearance. Mostly it seems like a cover story to explain runaway spouses and such.

"Long ago there was a story of a phantom chase leading to a murder near Spafford Creek. But I think it was a cover-up of vigilante violence against a vagrant. We once had a pretty rough crowd here in Lafayette County.

"Next you have the goblins and ghouls. These are your most hideous types. Goblins are usually bizarrely ugly and have the ability to stretch and distort themselves. They make big efforts to scare through these tactics.

"Ghouls are more passive. Their hideous looks come from horrible mutilations. So they usually just stand there with their guts hanging out or chopped off arms or maggot-filled eye sockets.

"I heard of goblins associated with caves and sink-holes. And the old people associated the goblins with hand-dug wells, root cellars, cisterns, and crawl spaces. Now if you think about it, it's a good tradition to keep alive if you want to keep kids out of dangerous places.

"But I know of at least a few that adults really believed in. One up by Yellowstone in an old springhouse. Then another in some old tumbled-down structure near Seymour Corners. A limekiln or something.

"Ghouls fall into two sub-categories. Of these, the cemetery ghouls are the most common. But they are not to be confused with your common cemetery ghost. No, cemetery ghouls are more than restless spirits, they're almost always the result of grave robbing and corpse mutilation.

"The other type of ghoul you might call the hidden grave ghoul. These are not in graveyards. These result from bodies stuffed in bricked-in fireplaces and under house foundations and other such hidden spots.

"Lafayette County does not have the tradition of cemetery ghouls that some places do. Check out Rock Island. I have one that I'm trying to verify up at Leslie near Belmont.

"But we have quite a few hidden grave ghouls. You might say Darlington is the capital of hidden grave ghouls. That goes back to that rough crowd I mentioned.

"During the Civil War and up to the turn of the century there were some pretty strange things going on. Lynchings and such. I guess no Gypsy, Jew, or Negro was safe in those days.

"It was said in Darlington that one tavern was built on a foundation of dead colored. The old jail also was supposed to have piles of bodies under the foundation.

"The peculiar thing about those Darlington ghouls is that no one sees them except the descendants of the wrongdoers from the old days. They're all from what were called 'copperhead' families, whatever that means.

"So what is seen as the harmless courthouse ghost by some is seen as a blood-and-pus-dripping lump of bullwhipped hobo by a few others.

"Then there are the wispy ghosts. These are the apparitions, wraiths, shades, shadows, and gossamers. You can barely make these out.

"I think this is where you get the idea of the bed sheet ghost. But as far as I can tell, most are seen as a whiff of smoke. And some are described as ladies or girls in white nighties. These don't seem to follow any firm pattern, although some seem to associate them with mansions and hotels and connect them to maids, cooks, and servant girls.

"I don't think that holds though, because there's a whole breed of wispy ghosts that I call the state line ghosts. They aren't all female and they are scattered in a variety of places.

"They run from Martintown in Green County to Apple River to Sinsinawa and East Dubuque. I don't claim to totally understand them yet. But they seem to have some connection to the borderline itself.

"An oldtimer from Hazel Green years ago told me a complicated story about these state line ghosts. He threw in stuff about the Northwest Ordinance, the survey point of beginning, and early inaccurate maps.

"From what he told me there was a miscalculation about where the south shore of Lake Michigan was and that the Illinois line was supposed to be drawn off that point. So there was a 20 mile wide strip of Illinois that should be in Wisconsin. This caused all sorts of havoc in the old deeds and surveys, I guess. And I guess for a long time it was common to have farms with land in both states.

"The Hazel Green oldtimer said this led to a group of malcontents who wanted to form a separate state called 'Winnebago.' They tried to drum up hysteria about Illinois becoming a slave state.

"But I still can't make much of a connection out of this mish-mash. Except that these borderline wispy ghosts are seen mostly on the roads that run right on the border.

"That's it for the main types and names. But Lafayette County also has a pile of one-of-a-kind ghosts that don't neatly fit these types.

"We have some isolated ethnic type ghosts. A German poltergeist and an Irish banshee. Some Swiss, Norwegian, and Scottish stuff too.

"But then there's the really odd stuff. In the White Oak area there was a tale of an 'outhouse goober.' Only they used the cruder word for outhouse. This was a Mulcahy Mine story and the details are pretty much lost to us today. But it seems this fellow could switch from type to type.

"We also have a Belmont Mound 'sentinel.' Like the name indicates, he just stands there and looks. It could be an Indian holdover.

"Finally, there's the Meekers Grove 'shifter.' This one changes from man to dog to deer to horse. Maybe other things too.

"There's other little tales, too. If you dig, you'll find one for every crossroads, hill, and abandoned homestead. The ghosts are everywhere."

Darlington's Courthouse Ghost

MANY OF THE stories in this collection illustrate how following the trail of one tale can lead to others. The stories also reveal story-collecting techniques that range from detective work to tavern "lubrication," from pure happenstance to naughty eavesdropping.

But the story of Darlington's Courthouse Ghost was unique in that I had to listen to hours of Lafayette County history and lore to get anywhere close to an explanation about the ghost. Along the way I had to pierce veil after veil of falsehood, self-deception, and cover-up.

Something bad happened in Darlington. Although the trail has grown cold as to the "facts," there remains a strong feeling of something horribly wrong, and of dark secrets.

One source explained this sinister maze as "the self-protective web of lies that we've woven so that we can't learn the truth."

The story here was drawn from discussions of a group of Lafayette County men who meet regularly for breakfast and storytelling. The remarks about the Courthouse Ghost flow from a more general report on courthouse history and rejoinders to that presentation.

The result is a somewhat disjointed tale. The members of this round-table have difficulty allowing an uninterrupted presentation. Abrupt questions, rude comments, and off-color catcalls are par for the course with this group. The chaos made it difficult to attribute many of the remarks to identifiable individuals.

Bear with us as we navigate the rapids of this raucous gathering.

Robert gave all the appearances of a plodding man. He paused for a considerable interval even though it was his turn to talk. A few snickers punctuated this silence.

Finally he shifted his considerable weight in his chair. The chair creaked. His thick fingers drummed the table in slow motion. He looked around the table and made eye contact with each of the group's regulars. His passive look turned to anger as he launched into a list of complaints about the group's failure to assist his investigation of courthouse history. Crude noises and a few profanities came back in reply.

With these frustrations off his chest he proceeded to run through discoveries and unanswered questions about the courthouse.

It became apparent that building the Lafayette County courthouse was a source of controversy and conflict in an earlier day. Shullsburg, Avon, and Hamilton were rivals as alternative sites. The dispute was quite bitter and progressed to high levels of rhetorical and physical confrontation. Inflammatory editorials and pamphlets were only slightly more common than fist-fights and threats of greater violence.

"The parties to this dispute raised all sorts of strange issues," said Robert. "They made all sorts of references to railroad monopolies, federal money policy, commodity prices, and banking policy. Even the Recon-struction policy in the South was thrown into the dispute."

Robert also spoke about court challenges and election campaigns. He said there were years of litigation and repeated referenda and counter-referenda.

"We had carpetbaggers coming in and bribes from businesses in Iowa County and Grant County. Voter fraud. Phony petitions. Non-resident voters. Intimidation and assault at polling places. Ballot box stuffing. Maybe even some kidnapping or disappearances."

In the midst of these troubling accounts, Robert also found humor. Apparently one early courthouse fight involved the desire of the local circus promoters, the Parson Brothers, to exhibit a buffalo in the courthouse.

As for the ghost, Robert felt this part of the story was at the core of the alleged cover-up. "Never before was a new building so quickly inhabited by ghosts. Supposedly the place had a ghost while still under construction."

A hooted comment suggested that disappearances during the rough and tumble competition for the courthouse site could be linked to any such construction phase ghost.

"Perhaps," conceded Robert.

"There was also talk of a worker killed during construction. And another story of someone killed by a runaway team with a wagon of building material. Anyway, there was wide agreement that there were fatalities associated with the building phase. Yet the local newspapers carried nothing about such events."

Several snorts of derision were thrown in at this point. A wisecrack about "conspiracy nuts" was thrown in by way of a lewd pun.

Robert plodded on. "Let's have a little dignity," he scolded mildly. "On this ghost stuff—and I know it's all in good fun—let's at least get the absurd stuff out of the way. Let's put to rest the Abraham Lincoln story.

"I don't know how many times I've had youngsters ask me about Abe Lincoln's ghost in the courthouse. Really! I don't know if one of you rascals started that foolish rumor. I know it's a recent invention. The ghost stories go way back. But this Lincoln thing you don't hear until more recent times. There's just no justification for it. It's either an imported story stolen out of Springfield, Illinois, or it's a plant to serve someone's agenda. Maybe an invention of one of the secret societies."

More hoots. More imitation of bodily noises. More ridicule of conspiracy theories. Plus an offensive suggestion that President Lincoln possessed an unnatural affection for young slave boys.

At this point one of the other men at the table rose to Robert's defense. "Lafayette County was a hotbed of secret societies," insisted a fellow named Jonathan. He said that there were a dozen or more groups in Lafayette County, conceding that many were harmless.

But he also spoke of a group called the Knights of the Golden Circle. This group he characterized as pro-Confederate southern sympathizers.

He felt it was a forerunner of the Ku Klux Klan. In addition he saw the group as a shadow organization within the Wisconsin Democrats' Nineteenth Century political organization.

Jonathan's report on this group wound through their disloyal acts during the Civil War to vigilante activity during a sixty-year period after the Civil War. He laid a number of covered-up murders and lynchings on their doorstep. He further linked everyone at the table to an ancestor with a Golden Circle connection.

The courthouse ghost, he reasoned, was the victim of one such lynching. He had evidence to suggest that a vagrant wrongly accused of a rape was pulled from the jail and lynched by a Golden Circle mob.

Robert concurred with this version. "That is pretty much the way I see it," he nodded. "I've seen the ghost. So have many others. And it doesn't really bother most people.

"Mostly it appears in the upper windows at night. Or cruises the ground floor hall.

"But the ghost is also a curse. A curse on those who have not admitted and rejected this dark past. The curse weighs heavy on this county and on many at this table. You know as well as I do that Lafayette County had not had good luck.

"But there is a way out of this curse. All the people of Lafayette County will have to do is collectively perform an act of compassion for outsiders.

"Not likely, is it?"

Part Six

Richland County

Gillingham Barn Poltergeist

BARNS OCCUPY A special niche in Wisconsin folklore. Barns are dairy-land castles which invoke a whole range of images about rural life.

Barn stories abound in southwest Wisconsin, where some of the oldest and finest barns grace the landscape. There are barn dance stories, barn wedding stories, barn funeral stories, and even barn murder stories.

One might expect that barn ghosts would pop up on every lonely stretch of county or town road. Not so.

Barn ghosts are comparatively rare. Southwest Wisconsin produced about two dozen leads on barn ghosts but only five of those proved to be anything other than boys with flashlights. Four of the remaining five seem to be one-time sightings of apparently itinerant ghosts seeking lodging in barns.

The fifth story is the only barn ghost with deep roots that I have found thus far.

A little speculation on this scarcity of barn ghosts might be in order. There are hints that area residents are especially tight-lipped about such spirits.

After all, the barn is revered on the farm and as many hours might be spent there as in one's house. The reader will note that the ghost stories openly discussed by sources are usually in public places or abandoned buildings. It seems that ghosts in one's private space are viewed more intimately and are seldom discussed with strangers.

Then, too, barns have evolved in southwest Wisconsin. The earliest pioneer structures are extremely rare. Fire and storms have claimed many. Changing needs and growing herd sizes have swept away many old-style hay mow barns. Finally, abandonment has left many barns to the fate of collapse.

Many preservationists claim that the barn is an endangered building form. Perhaps ghosts feel that way too.

The home of Gillingham's barn ghost is in good shape. The barn is in the hands of the same German-American family who built it over a century ago. It is well maintained and freshly painted.

It was used for milking up until the late 1970s. It was then converted to hold grandchildren's horses and 4-H lambs.

Because of privacy concerns and a desire to keep traffic off their long one-lane access road, the family has asked that the location be kept vague. Let's just say the barn is south of Spring Hill Road and north of Cribben Hill.

※　※　※

"The barn's been haunted ever since it was built," insisted Evelyn.

"My great-grandfather built it soon after he came to America. Our family was lumped in with Bohemians but they spoke German. Great-grandfather died shortly after it was built. He might be buried under these big pines north of the barn.

"People in the neighborhood always suggested that the ghost was Great-grandfather or somebody else in the family. But that's not so. The old people in the family were quite insistent that the ghost was an old-fashioned German poltergeist. A noisy, cane-raising ghost, full of tricks."

The family charted the ghost's history along with the evolution of the barn.

"Like a lot of old barns, it was really built in stages," said her husband.

"The first stage was a log crib barn. Then they covered it with metal sheathing and made it into a grainery. The center part came next when putting up a lot of hay became a concern.

"Then came the big hip shed out back. More machinery meant more space needs. Finally they built the addition with calf pens, horse stalls, and a milkhouse. It's always been said that the poltergeist moved into each new addition as soon as it was finished to christen it with a prank.

"Oh, how I wish you could have heard Evelyn's father's stories. He had hundreds of them about the poltergeist.

"He always spoke fondly of the poltergeist. It was almost like he was talking about a high-spirited son whose sins and faults were overlooked.

"There were common pranks and unique ones. Common things like the milk going sour right in the pail. Or full milk cans mysteriously emptying.

"On the unique side there was the real corker with the weathervane. The poltergeist had the direction pointer going round and round in a blurry spin for days.

"But usually it was things like cows kicking like they'd been goosed. Or buckets and cans rattling out little tunes. And the thing they looked forward to around Christmas time when the poltergeist would play Christmas carols on the cows' bells.

"My favorite was the trick the poltergeist reserved for the hired men. They were often made to slip so they'd land face down in the cowpies.

"I can't say as there's anything too dramatic going on in the barn these days. It's not like before. With the poltergeist or us for that matter.

"It use to be the barn was a place of daily laughter. Kids learned about life out there. I heard prayers said in that barn. I know of courting that went on there.

"Now the poltergeist might unhook a door or tip over a pile of bales. But I get some comfort when I look out at that barn at night and see that the poltergeist has that kerosene lantern burning. He's welcome out there for as long as he wants."

The Windeeko Spirit of Pine River

Among the many ghost stories left behind by Wisconsin's original inhabitants is the legend of the Windeeko Spirit of Pine River. Known variously as windigos, wendikos, and wintikos, windeekos are not usually classified as ghosts. In Algonkian lore the windeeko is a monster figure sometimes cast as a demonic spirit.

This story is unusual in that it involves one form of supernatural being which is transformed into a ghost. There is a presumption of some sort of "death" that must account for this metamorphosis from monster to ghost.

The storyteller here offers theories about this unique transformation. But the story remains an oddity even within the realm of odd occurrences.

🌿 🌿 🌿

Bright glints of light were thrown up off the rippling waters at the Pine River boatlanding. It was night on the Wisconsin River, a moonless and purple dark sky. The light on the ripples of the meeting currents of the Pine and the Wisconsin was from a driftwood fire on the shore.

A hint of autumn spiced the air of the summer night. By the fire three fishermen grunted and sipped cans of Special Export.

They were one of those oddly-matched groups that invite speculation. A coach and two assistants? A bishop and two priests?

Everything about them—from beard stubble on faces accustomed to daily shaving (the constant rubbing gave them away) to pricey Eddie Bauer duds proudly encrusted with fish slime and dirt—said non-locals.

They were not really fishing. "Just practicing, just chanting the mantra," said the heavy one in the UW-Stevens Point sweatshirt.

A tall companion whittled large slivers off a sun-bleached stick.

The most senior of the trio watched the water. He did not take his eyes off the ripples, even when he spoke. "Have you heard of the spirit who lives out here?"

"It's a common story in a way. But not commonly understood. I grew up near here. That was a long time ago. Even then there were stories. But not so they made much sense.

"You often have to leave home so that you can come back and have things make sense. You often need somebody outside your family to give you a fresh view of familiar things."

The older fisherman paused, picked up a stick, stirred the coals of the fire, and then threw the stick out toward the spot he was watching. His eyes never left the ripples of the confluence of the water.

"A fresh view of things. That's the key to understanding just about everything.

"When I was a boy you just heard little snippets. They said there's an evil thing on the Pine River. They said be careful out there. They said strange things happen out there.

"If you were the curious sort you'd ask what they meant by all that. The old folks would just glare at you as if you were challenging them. Oh, then they might whip off with some remark about somebody going crazy. It never made a lot of sense.

"Then about twenty years ago I was back on a visit. Well, actually wrapping up a family estate. Just on a whim I came out here on an evening drive. Hadn't thought of the place in years. An old boy had a fire going right here on this spot. Funny looking, wiry old man with a patch over one eye. He told me he was a Spanish-American War veteran.

"I didn't buy it because that would have made him darn near a hundred years old. He was old. But he was Lucky Strike cigarette and Wild Turkey whiskey old. He asked me if I knew about the spirit. I told him I had heard plenty of nonsense.

"Then he told me to sit down and receive my true education. I laughed at that because the old boy never came closer to a degree than a first-degree burn. But the old boy wasn't fazed by my laugh. He just starting telling the tale.

"He said there was a Windeeko—an ogre of some kind—right here off the mouth of the Pine River. He said the Windeeko was created when the last chunk of glacier floated down the Wisconsin River and was jammed up on a rock that was here in those days. The ice turned into the monster.

"This Windeeko terrorized all living things in the area for thousands of years. It sucked canoes under the water. It ate whole herds of animals. It blighted the crops and blew in summer blizzards.

"Finally the Sauk moved into the area. They sent many warriors against the Windeeko, but none of them returned.

"The Sauk chiefs met for many days trying to figure out what to do next. They came up with the idea to send their old medicine man.

"The medicine man had no idea how to deal with this monster. So he thought he would just hide here and study the Windeeko. He learned about the shifting sands here. He also determined that the big rock was magical.

"Then the idea come to him. He called out the Windeeko. He told the Windeeko that he had come to be killed but that first he wanted to see just how strong the Windeeko was. So he asked that the Windeeko lift the big rock out of the water.

"The Windeeko hefted the rock up in the air. But the massive weight of the big rock caused him to slide down into the hole at the mouth of the Pine River. The Windeeko tipped over backwards. The rock drove him to the bottom of the deep hole and pinned him there. The monster was crushed. But in a last scream that was heard in Canada the Windeeko placed a curse on the Sauk.

"The old boy offered several theories about what had happened. The Windeeko was turned into a ghost right away and set to work on the curse. Or the monster went dormant and was only activated as a river spirit when the settlers came. He even offered an explanation that the coming of the first Jesuits down the River stirred up this ghost.

"So the spirit is out there laying at the bottom of that hole. So it doesn't have its old mobility. But it can affect things nearby. It can exert power over the minds of those who travel over that spot. In fact, you could say it can move into those minds and set up housekeeping.

"I was pretty skeptical about this. But the old boy gave me a demonstration. He fashioned a cross out of sticks and threw it out there on the ripples. The water started to boil!

"What do you make of that?

"For those who want proof I offer the fate of the Sauk. I also ask that they consider the weird things along the lower Wisconsin River. Accidents, bodies dumped, people going crazy.

"The old boy told me one more thing. He said one day the Windeeko spirit would be put to rest and that a new age would dawn.

"You might say I'm waiting on that."

Lone Rock's Artillery Ghosts

THE SOUTHEAST RICHLAND County community of Lone Rock has a high per capita rate of ghost stories. The main one is the Wisconsin River "lorelei" included in the Iowa County chapter because of its association with the cliffs on the south bank of the river. But one can find references to dozens of hauntings.

Perhaps the tri-county borders lead to confusion over ownership of these various tales that in turn is a disincentive to flesh out the details of the stories. What's the deal on the Bakken Pond Ghost? Why do people over at Clyde think that Long Island is haunted? Why is the spirit of an old aviator in a biplane seen at the Tri-County Airport? What is behind the strange glowing red eyes out on Old Mill Road and Bear Creek?

Well, in Lone Rock they will not answer those questions. The most you can do on most of these tales is relate what you have heard and elicit a nod and a grunting "I've heard that too."

The exception to this tight-lipped behavior came in the form of a few remarks about the Lone Rock Artillery Ghosts.

Readers will recall the Soldiers Grove Phantoms of the Crawford County chapter and the reference there to the existence of many fragments of Civil War ghost stories.

Lone Rock residents are able to take this story beyond a mere fragment, but not by much. It is hard to find the sociology of this tale or any subtext of community values.

The story is included because of several unique features. First, the ghost themselves are never seen. Second, the sightings involve horses and equipment associated with the ghosts. And, finally, the bulk of the incidents involve sound rather than visual phenomena.

🌿 🌿 🌿

Lone Rock's artillery unit is the source of a reasonable amount of local pride. A dignified monument to the unit sits in an enclosed area in the middle of town along Highway 130.

Younger residents know very little about the monument or the unit. Their elders lament the disappearance of the standard one-room school curriculum on Civil War history.

The monument is notable for its complete listing of unit members. Visitors on family history missions often stop to check names.

There is a considerable amount of local folklore about the unit, its exploits, and leadership. Local reference is always to the "Lone Rock Artillery" rather than the formal designation of the Sixth Wisconsin Artillery.

As it turns out, not all members of the Sixth were Lone Rock residents. Surrounding areas of Richland, Sauk, Iowa, and even Grant counties contributed volunteers to the unit.

The Sixth was commanded by Captain Henry Dillon. Local legend often promotes him to the rank of colonel or general and labels him a hero of Gettysburg and Antietam.

Yet the monument itself clearly puts the Sixth in the western part of the war. Vicksburg and Corinth are emblazoned in large stone letters which suggest memories of horror and depravation.

Regardless of the gap between local folklore and historical fact, the Sixth lives on in strange ways.

"I've heard the artillery about a dozen times," claimed Ben, the bartender.

"It's about six cannons going off in a row. You know, boom, boom, boom, boom, boom, boom! A quick volley, then quiet.

"A lot of people around here say they've never heard the cannons. Or they say it was just thunder."

While the sound is something that has been heard for over a hundred years the location has shifted with time. Initially the cannons were heard to sound off right at the monument location. Sometime around seventy years ago the site of the firing moved out of the village.

Recent accounts place the firing mainly on the bluffs north of County Line Road and on Long Island. However, a few people insist that the sound is more distant.

The physical sightings are rarer but still common enough to pose a number of variations.

The classic sightings are those involving the full complement of equipment.

"I've seen the whole deal go through town," beamed one townsman.

"Heavy black horses pulling those hitchcarts that pull the cannons. Whatday call them? Caissons, yeah. Well, first come the horses, caissons, and cannons. Then come the heavy wagons with extra shot and shell. Finally there's the wheelwright, blacksmith, and farrier wagon for repair needs.

"Not a single driver or rider on any of them. Though I could have swore I saw the lines or reins pulled up without slack as if somebody was there."

But often as not the sightings involve only bits and pieces of the artillery column. Sometimes there were only horses with harnesses taut as if the equipment is there. Other times it is the caissons and wagons which are seen without the animals. One source reports only a line of wagon wheels.

Unlike the accounts of cannon fire, the sightings all follow the same path. The cannons and horses always come into Lone Rock from the east off old Kennedy Road and turn north through the town on Highway 130. They never get as far as Highway 14.

The sightings are always after midnight. The hour of 3 a.m. seems to be the peak observation time. A large number of sightings come after heavy storms when the street lights have been knocked out by lightning.

The locals attach no particular significance to the sightings or sounds. In the voices of the storytellers you can sense a bit of innocent pride and amusement.

"It's something that makes Lone Rock special," points out the bartender. It's something to talk about besides the weather and milk prices. It's a good thing to have a connection to history like that. Besides nobody ever got scared. Those artillery ghosts don't bother a soul. A sound sleeper sleeps right through the whole deal."

Rockbridge's Wraith

The picturesque country along Richland County's stretch of Highway 80 is a natural setting for folklore and strange tales. Perhaps no portion of that road evokes the possibility of powerful unseen forces more than the stone bluffs that run north from Buck Creek, through Rockbridge, and up past Hub City.

The more pious of the area's residents marvel at the Creator's landscaping experiments. The local wags credit the Devil. Many find the rock formations to be both visually pleasing and yet somehow threatening.

No precise explanation of the threat is given. Just vague comments about something watching, lurking, and looming.

This stretch of the upper Pine River valley is fertile territory for tales about Kickapoo Indians, Black Hawk, early loggers, and stubborn homesteaders.

Ghost stories are common, too. No shortage of haunted one-room school houses, sawmills and taverns here.

As with so much rural lore, the details on these Pine River valley ghosts are sparse. The generation that knows the stories between the sightings is fast disappearing.

The Rockbridge Wraith can be distinguished from these run-of-the-mill ghost stories. First, the use of the term "wraith" makes it unusual in Wisconsin. "Wraith" is an uncommon ghost label more likely to be found in New England or the Pacific Northwest. It conjures up images of gauzy and frail spirits floating on the drafts of abandoned mansions. There is also some connection to the leading maritime families of small port towns.

In addition, it is clearly a female figure. As readers of this collection will notice, feminine spirits seem to be in short supply. My advisers attribute this gender imbalance to the greater incidence of violent male death and their greater amounts of unresolved business.

Be that as it may, the Rockbridge Wraith represents an interesting feminist slant on pioneer life.

It is easy enough to find reports of the Rockbridge Wraith gliding the tops of rock outcroppings between Steamboat Hollow and Soules Creek. It is a bit more difficult to probe local feelings about this ghost. A stop at a Rockbridge yard sale yielded up one interesting interpretation.

🌿 🌿 🌿

"Our wraith belongs to the ladies," smiled the small woman in the broad straw hat.

"The men used to tell the story, but it always came out like nonsense. They whittled her down to a sweet young thing in a flimsy nightgown. Typical.

"It is true that she's always in a nightgown. But it's nothing daring. It's one of those old-fashioned, buttoned-at-the-neck, ankle-length, plain white nightgowns. Basically the same thing women wore for hundreds of years before pajamas.

"She is an attractive young woman in an unworldly way. She has a delicate frame and creamy features.

"There is a lot of debate about who she is and how she got here. There is no doubt in my mind that at least one family around here is hiding some big secrets.

"I've heard so much about her I don't believe ninety percent of it. Especially the bar talk. Things like her being a runaway who became a saloon girl. Or that she was a nun who had a baby.

"From what I can tell—and that all comes from my Great Aunt Dorothy—there were two families involved in this story. Dorothy was pretty sure that it was the Ryans and the Cribbens but she never got their roles straight.

"Now our wraith was not a Ryan or a Cribben. She was a stranger. Dorothy said from back east.

"She came out as a mail-order bride. She was supposed to marry a farmer from one of the two families. But she soon saw that the farmer was an older rough man and that she was in for a hard life.

"Even in life she was a frail little thing. Not at all suited to a pioneer wife's chores and child-bearing. She tried to do her duty. But her rough husband made her life harder rather than easier. On top of all his other crudeness, he was a mean man with an evil temper.

"A young man in the other family noticed her welts and bruises. Maybe he offered her comfort or refuge. Maybe it was romantic interest. But it started a scandal and a family feud. And after her husband retrieved her the beatings intensified.

"No one thinks she was actually beaten to death. But her already poor health was ground down until she had no will to live. She was mourned with a sense of shame upon everyone who failed to help her.

"After that, her spirit started its wandering. She's usually seen in moonlight traveling the cliff tops where the pines grow. But she is also seen peeking out of caves.

"That would be enough of a story. And I know a few people who've been scared by her moonlight walks. But there is another part. Something that is whispered about but not admitted in public. She also makes visits to some men around here. She's an evening caller if you get my meaning.

"She leaves the good family men and innocent boys alone. She seeks out the unfaithful, and the abusers.

"In this role she doesn't just drift down off the cliff in her nightie. These men don't see her in her usual form. She comes to them as a floozy. All that the men see is a new face with easy virtues.

"This happens mainly in the taverns of Hub City—places that a Christian lady like me has never set foot in. Similar things are said to happen in the taverns of Bloom City, La Farge, and Cazenovia.

"It is probably not a coincidence that all those communities have descendants of the two families. But I won't go so far as to say that all of her visits are with relatives of those families. I think she'll pay a visit on almost any man who thinks he's God's gift to women or any man who thinks women are punching bags.

"When the noses of these low life dogs catch her scent, they're hooked. She can easily seduce them. Then off they go. Either to park in a car or to some greasy cot in a hunting shack.

"That's when they get their surprise. They start to have physical relations with what appears to be a young woman. Then comes the change. In the middle of this lewd business she changes into a ghoulish hag. A hag with a grip of iron who won't let go of them.

"They say that some of these low-lifes are not right in the mind after this experience. Some have been taken away in straitjackets.

"But those may be the lucky ones. The ones that go crazy. The unlucky ones lose part of their maleness. Papa never let the girls into the barn when he turned the bull calves into steers—but we heard them cry. Our wraith may not be strong—but she's quick with her little knife."

Part Seven

Vernon County

Wildcat Mountain's Sentinel

SEVERAL STORIES IN this collection owe debts to broader folktale origins. But eastern Vernon County has a very distinctive folklore tradition which draws upon a history of self-reliance and more recent conflicts with authority.

There is an almost Appalachian feel evoked by Wildcat Mountain and Mount Pisgah. Travelers speak glowingly of mystery and scenic beauty along Highway 131 from LaFarge to Ontario.

Local residents appreciate the natural wonders but also feel a sense of struggle with nature. A mood of hard times lingers in the air.

Hard feelings against bureaucrats are fairly common in rural areas. However, along the upper Kickapoo the distrust is as profound as any found in Wisconsin.

This preface to a ghost story is not the place to air political grievances. Suffice it to say that decades of federal duplicity on the Kickapoo dam project and farm credit problems have built deep resentments toward government. These attitudes leave an indelible mark on this treasure tale about a lost gold shipment on Wildcat Mountain.

A long time Rockton resident speaks in a voice filled with anger.

🌿 🌿 🌿

"There's a treasure up on Wildcat Mountain. Did you know that? Most people don't!

"The government knows. They don't want anybody else to get it. Get the gold, I mean! Gold like you won't believe. Bags and bags of it. Worth millions, I would guess. Not that I'd want to share any."

My source then went on to explain the origins of the legends surrounding Wildcat Mountain. He spoke of a Billings family and a Montana connection. He pointed out the existence of a local Cheyenne Valley. The story involved a load of gold in an iron-plated wagon. The Billings boys and ten armed guards brought the wagon back from out West.

Somehow there was a connection to Governor Altgeld of Illinois, William Jennings Bryan, and some Oklahoma radicals. Mention was also made of shadowy groups and odd conspiracies.

"Somehow the word about the gold got out," he hissed. "I guess you can't keep a thing like that secret. Before long outlaws were after the gold and the government too. As if there's much difference between those two type of thieves.

"I guess we had the whole she-bang. Treasury agents, Army spies, U.S. marshalls, congressional investigators, and even postal inspectors. A bunch of gutter creatures who never did an honest day's work and had no talent except for minding other people's business.

"But the Billings boy pulled a fast one. The gold was taken off the wagon and buried on Wildcat Mountain. Then the wagon and the guards continued on."

My source then explained that Latin American revolutions and World War One claimed the lives of everyone who had seen where the gold was buried. However, he claimed that clues were left behind in the form of letters written by the Billings boy. The letters contained obscure references to astronomy, astrology, and mythology.

When he originally told me the story of the lost treasure he de-emphasized the ghost elements. This was probably because of confusion on his part.

In his first telling he referred to multiple "ghost sentries." He also spoke of horse sounds, sounds of fighting, and a wildcat spirit as things separate and apart from the treasure story.

But some cross-checking and prodding from me prompted a few amendments and clarifications on his part.

"I've re-thought what I told you. Talked to few others I know. And I guess it's really only one ghost guarding the gold.

"It could be that all their strange stories, noises, and odd things at Wildcat Mountain are from this one ghost. I never really thought about this possibility before. But I guess it's logical. How can you expect a man to think clearly about that stuff when there might be millions in gold laying around?

"Let's get some things straight first. I thought better of telling you about this for awhile. I don't really need competition for the treasure from a bunch of wide-eyed stumblebums looking for ghosts.

"But this sentinel doesn't stand on top of the gold. So when people see this ghost they aren't going to find anything. That's the whole point, he decoys them away! The ghost throws people off the trail so to speak.

Unless you have some clues where to look and unless you have some knowledge about how to neutralize ghosts.

"I don't have to worry about amateurs poking around. If some poor fool manages to dig a hole up there, the DNR and tax boys will be on him so quick. Hell, 'til the lawyers get done with it, the sorry S.O.B. will be in jail or the poorhouse!

"You wanted to know what kind of things this ghost does? I've heard dozens of different stories! The most common is thrown rocks out of thin air. Quite often right up side the head of snoops. I've actually seen that happen.

"A couple of people had the bejeebers scared out of them when the ghost chased after them with a big bowie knife. One nearsighted old boy said it was a sword. But that's not likely. This ghost is more of a roughrider or cowboy.

"Some have seen him on horseback. On a sturdy cavalry mount. Others see him standing out on rocks with a rifle. That's how I've seen him.

"Lots of oldtimers say that the ghost has a thirty-forty krag. A Spanish-American War gun. But I've seen something that looks like a fifty-caliber buffalo gun.

"Plenty of times people don't see a thing. Sometimes it's just the sound of a horse bearing down on them. Often it's a push from behind that tumbles them over a log or stump.

"The horse sounds are often heard from some distance. The ghost gallops that horse from the base of the mountain right to the top.

"Then there's the really strange stuff. About the ghost appearing as an animal. One minute someone will see the ghost up on a rock. Then he's gone. Next thing they're being charged by some wild thing. Sometimes it's a bear. Sometimes it's a bull. I heard one claim of a buffalo. That was the nearsighted old boy who saw the sword, though.

"Most often it's a wildcat. That's what I saw. Now some people don't know what a wildcat is. So there's been all sorts of confusion about bobcats, lynx, and mountain lions. The DNR feeds this problem with their mountain lion and wolf stories. It's the DNR plan to get country people scared so they can buy up the land.

"But I saw the wildcat. Now some say this form of the ghost goes way back. Back before the gold. I've seen the wildcat. He changes his size from house-cat size to big old Buick size. But sometimes you see just the shadow and not the cat himself.

"I saw him on the full run on Highway 131 one night. I followed him from the Hay Valley Road junction down into the Town of Stark until he bounded off on Plum Run Road just before La Farge. Lucky there was no traffic. He ran down the centerline!

"There's not much else to say. Some suspect that the ghost is behind local accidents. But that could be government stuff. They want to turn Vernon County into a park. And a big poison landfill too. And they'll train foreign troops here too.

"Now I have nothing against those fellows who work at the park. Some of them seem decent. But if any pointy-head from Madison or Washington were to lay a finger on so much as a nickel of this treasure, well, I'd see that S.O.B. in hell!

"And I'd have some help from that ghost. You betcha!"

Hillsboro's Exorcist

OUR JOURNEY THROUGH southwest Wisconsin shows us that strange stories about the supernatural are not in short supply. But tales with an overtly occult side to them are not common.

It is true that here and there an odd occurrence might be attributed to sorcery or that an older eccentric person might be labeled a witch. Yet it is difficult to find the types of integrated views of the supernatural and the "black arts" that one detects in Irish and German folklore. American supernatural folklore is more fragmented and seldom rises to the level of a "system."

Hillsboro harbors a story that hints at this systems approach. The source of the tale is a local businessman whose respectable and conventional reputation is in sharp contrast to the way of life described here.

"It was my grandfather," Oliver started.

"My dad's dad. He had peculiar ways and ideas. Sometimes it's hard to imagine that we grew up in a family like that.

"He was called an exorcist. But I'm not sure that is the proper name. We weren't Catholics and grandfather had never studied these matters from a theological background.

"But I can't think of a better name. Sorcerer, alchemist, medicine man, or hex doctor? They're all inadequate to describe the breadth of his approach. It ranged from fairly accepted herbal folk medicine to potions, charms, lifting of curses, and driving away evil spirits. The Native Americans have a name that sort of gets at it: Shaman. The locals just stuck with the label exorcist.

"The practice was hidden from view. The general public did not really know about it. Only the older people knew much about it.

"I never heard of anything quite like it anywhere else. But then again, as a stranger you wouldn't know about such things in other communities. The Amish up this way have some healers, but that's more Bible-based. I don't think they deal with supernatural activities.

"Grandfather's views touched every aspect of life. He saw very little that was not in need of healing.

"I don't want you to get the idea that he was chasing bogeymen across the countryside. He just thought that there was a balance necessary to life. And that balance would come only when evil was put on the defensive. He was not one of your 'everything is relative' liberal types. He saw evil in the world and viewed himself as a soldier—hell, a general—in the fight against evil.

"Not just big time end-of-the-world, Antichrist, Horsemen-of-the-Apocalypse-type evil. But the kinds that poison communities and keep people from experiencing the joy that should be the human birthright.

"So grandfather dealt with livestock problems. Or where to locate a well. Or when to plant a certain crop or when to go fishing. He was a repository of all sorts of practical knowledge. And as he grew old I think he came to typify the patience and tolerance that must be the foundation of all wisdom.

"Patience and tolerance may not sound like character traits of someone single-minded about waging war on evil. But it was part and parcel of his compassion for the young, the disadvantaged, and the ignorant.

He saved his fire and brimstone for the genuinely malignant forces which he saw lurking behind evil deeds.

"He studied old manuscripts, legends, and religions of many countries. All in an effort to understand the nature of evil.

"But his views were also shaped by both sides of the family. His granddad was an old Scotchman filled with stories of dragons and haunted caverns. His mother was of was of rural German stock, Alsatians, actually, and she was a walking library of peasant folk knowledge."

The businessman went on to explain how his grandfather had drawn upon those family sources to develop a compendium of evil and malignant forces. This dictionary of magic was organized in reverse alphabetical order.

The individual entries in this listing gave definitions, types of behavior, and recommendations on charms, amulets, and cures. Most information was thought to be hundreds if not thousands of years old. However, the businessman did admit that his grandfather created a few to deal with crises that fit no established formula.

Many of these magical prescriptions were meant to be read in chant-like fashion. Others were simply recipes. Ethnic connections and national origin were also listed, if known.

The businessman's grandfather thought that it was essential to know the lineage of the spirit or demon and the ethnic heritage of those afflicted by such forces. The old exorcist said that there was power and deterrent value in knowing these forces and their modus operandi.

The businessman recited selected portions of the lists (quoting some from memory). Then he went on to explain specific applications of the information and how local spirits had been dealt with.

"Grandfather was sought out in his day. He went up to drive out spirits from a ship on Lake Superior. He often was called to Iowa and Minnesota. He told me that his toughest case was a local one. A Chaseburg church haunting. Multiple spirits, I recall.

"The pastor had many sins to atone for and had aggrieved many women if you catch my drift. Unfortunately he only confessed these things to grandfather one at a time.

"Grandfather said this lack of a whole picture kept him from dealing effectively with the situation. There were apparently twists and turns that kept him on this case over a year.

"The complications made grandfather a nervous wreck. There was a spirit in the church stove traceable to an oath uttered by the husband of one faithless woman. There was the crying of the spirit of a stillborn child. There were barking spirit dogs and spirit owls. There were incidents at services and funerals.

"Besides adultery and illegitimacy, it turned out there had been dipping into the collection plate, cheating of widows, and even some jewelry pilfering from the dead. The funny thing is, Grandfather had to go back to Chaseburg to drive the pastor's nuisance spirit out of the church after the corrupt clergyman died.

"Other than that, most of the things he talked about seemed like a craftsman's routine. He wasn't falsely modest. He would readily talk about his sense of accomplishment when he solved problems.

"He talked about dozens and dozens. Most I can't remember. Lots of little things, like locating a cursed nail in a barn that had soured the cows' milk.

"But as far as troublesome spirits, oh yes, there were some memorable ones. I think the first one he told me about was a haunted springhouse over by Westby on Unseth Road. He said he had to hang mirrors on all four sides and kept a lantern lit in there with the mirrors for thirteen nights.

"In Viroqua he dealt with a number of things. I remember a spirit who polluted cistern water—he smoked that one out. And there was some sort of violent haunting at a tobacco storage facility. It took an old Scottish spell to clear that place out.

"Bartons Corners had a strange one. They had an outhouse spirit there. It started at a farm on Grim Road. Grandfather drove it out of there with a special beeswax and sage candle. But it just moved down the road. So he had to remove it again and again in that vicinity. Then he chased it around Mount Tabor, Trippville, Dilly, White City, and Greenwood. That kept him busy for years. But I think he made out pretty well selling all those special candles.

"There was a spirit that bothered horses around Avalanche and Bloomingdale. He said something about a suppository he made for the horses. I can't remember what went into that concoction.

"Right here in Hillsboro we had two of his favorite cases. One was a haunted stable and blacksmith shop that he exorcised after a marathon hymn singing. The other was a possession of a young Bohemian girl. A goat had to be sacrificed and its blood painted in a circle around the girl.

"In Purdy there were strange cemetery eruptions. Yes, the ground pushing up like a bubbling stew. Some coffins were belched right out of the ground. That problem resulted from the foolish placement of graves in a prior burial ground.

"There were haunted bridges over by Stoddard and Genoa. Those were both Norwegian-related problems and were dispatched based on old Norse lore.

"One of the funnier ones was the possession of a five-hundred-pound boar hog in the Romance area on Cox Creek. The big animal did a lot of damage. It was eating poultry and dogs and cats in the area. People were even scared for the children.

"Grandfather's plan was to put a crucifix around its neck. The hog had other ideas. It took off and carried grandfather on a two-mile wild ride. But he hung on and dug the crucifix chain into the hog's neck. Eventually the oxygen shortage brought the hog down. Grandfather said the hog was a true Christian after that.

"He was also involved in that famous case up in Tomah. The one with the whole family of possessed children. But he didn't get the credit for saving them. It was really a joint effort with a priest, a Winnebago medicine woman, a gypsy, and a ninety-year-old Negro woman.

"Grandfather also saw his work in relation to other events and customs in the community. For example, he felt that lively Halloween festivities worked to minimize spirit problems, so he encouraged the young in their Halloween rowdiness.

"There were those—including those in local pulpits—who maintained that Grandfather stirred up ghost hysteria. Some said he practiced black magic to conjure up demons so he could profit from their removal.

"He did have good business sense. But he had an even better heart. He helped many people without any reward. And he continues to help even fifty years after death. But that's another story!"

The Kickapoo Polka Band

GHOSTLY MUSIC IS a fairly common occurrence in southwest Wisconsin. From the reports of a military band at Soldiers Grove, to faint banjo strumming at Pleasant Ridge, to echoes of alpenhorns at New Glarus, to sounds of a piano at a lonely Lafayette County school house, the auditory experience of music is part of the area's rich spirit world.

Vernon County's entry in this category stands out from other tales on several counts. In the other tales music is but one feature of a broader ghost encounter. In this story music is the sole manifestation of this group of spirits.

In addition, other musical ghosts have extremely limited repertoires, often limited to two or three songs or even a few bars of one song. The Vernon County experience is a virtual request line within a few musical genres.

The Kickapoo Polka Band came to my attention while researching folktales about dances held in Vernon County's distinctive round barns.

The reader will perhaps draw connections between the source's fondness for those dances of the past and her propensity to hear the music. However, a number of other sources (some far more cynical) provide at least partial corroboration.

🌿 🌿 🌿

"Oh, yes, I'll tell you about the ghost music," whispered Helen, the retired storekeeper.

"This is mostly a Vernon County story. Mostly in the area west of Highway 14. But I'll refer you to some other people who can bear me out.

"I'd say that Potts Corners seems to be the geographical center of this thing. But the leading places to hear the Kickapoo Polka Band are Buckeye Ridge and Sandhill Ridge.

"Oh, yes, it can be heard other places. There are stories from around Yuba and Woodstock in Richland County. Also Cashton in Monroe County and Newburg Corners in LaCrosse County. And as far south as

Montgomeryville in Crawford County. But mostly its our story right here in the center of Vernon County.

"Now when I first heard it I was visiting a cousin near Potts Corners. We were sitting on the porch having a lemonade. It was not quite dark. We heard the music come from on the other side of the woods. There wasn't a house over there, so we were a bit surprised.

"This was over forty years ago, so car radios and portable radios were not common around here. But our best guess at first was that it was a car radio.

"The thing was that the music was so lively and you could hear the individual instruments. You could even tell a few of the musicians weren't quite in time with the rest.

"Then the first song gave way to the next, then the next. So it wasn't a radio with commercials. And there was laughing and such. What a mystery!

"Eventually we just had to get in the car and drive over there. We drove back a neighbors tractor lane but couldn't see a thing. When we got out of the car there was nothing. Oh, my, the music was now coming from back over at my cousin's house.

"So we just drove back and sat on that porch and listened. We thought it was just one of those freaks of nature where sound carried a long way or where radio waves came out of a rock.

"We had the benefit of almost two hours of music. Then it quit. We laughed about our concert being over then turned our conversation to other things. It was getting late so I had to leave. Just as I got in the car the music started again. Their half hour break was over. My cousin and I laughed as I drove away.

"She later said the music went on another hour and a half. She tried to go to bed but it kept her up. And she heard it three or four more times that summer. I heard it there several times since then. But the next time I heard it was near Ontario.

"I was at a girlfriend's house. She and I were talking about the old barn dances, including the ones that took place in the old round barn on her farm. That barn had fallen down long before. Then through the kitchen window screen we heard the music. It was coming right from where the old barn boards lay in a pile in the foundation.

"When we went out the back door the music stopped. Then we went back to the kitchen table and the music started again. So we went to the door again. The music stopped again.

"We laughed about how we must be the old people now. In our younger days there was a lookout at a barn dance to report whether a parent or grandparent was coming.

"My girlfriend heard the band at least once a summer after that. For nearly thirty years until she passed away.

"After the Ontario experience I heard other reports of people hearing the music. I followed them up and was lucky enough to hear the music at over two dozen different places. Oh, my, I had adventures!

"The last new place for me was just three summers ago. My grandson took me to his little hunting shack on the back side of Buckeye Ridge. That night the music started later than usual. The music even seemed a little different. It was almost as if his presence and his age changed things.

"Before I get into more experiences I should mention things I've learned about the band. First, it seems to be a large band, beyond the three- or four-piece bands that were once common in the area.

"A good ear could hear at least three accordions, two guitars, two trumpets, a fiddle, and a tuba. Some claim to have heard a piano. I never did.

"But with my grandson I did hear a harmonica. The music was, what—little jazzy? Maybe with a colored sound to it? And my grandson later said he heard drums.

"This goes to show that my idea about the band is probably true. Some of the others who hear it try to guess which band from the old times now plays as ghosts. But I say it's not a band that played together when the musicians were alive. I think they're joined by whatever ghost musicians are available.

"Oh, my, the music! Just the sort of thing that had me on my feet as a girl. Polkas, waltzes, and even a few square dance tunes. They play all sorts of polkas. German, Polish, and Bohemian. Some that were even crossed up with Irish and Scottish music. There was even an element of what you might call country and western music. Tunes taken from Jimmy Rogers, Hank Williams, and Patsy Cline songs.

"Not that there was much singing. Usually just the instruments. What singing there was often sounded like other languages. That and some yodelling.

"You should know that not everyone calls them the Kickapoo Polka Band. That's the name that you hear in the eastern part of the county. Over by Viroqua they're called the Dutchmen. But that probably comes from the fact that so many polka bands had the word dutchmen in their names. I don't think any of them were really Dutch.

"You want to know if any of this is connected to the stories I told you about the round barns and the dances in them? Not really. The music has been heard near a couple old barns. But mostly its been heard coming out of woods, hillsides, and valleys. Even a church pavilion and empty veterans hall.

"No, the round barns were just a special piece of community life. They were good for dancing in a circle. And the barn dances helped bring people together. It was the best way to get to know others outside your own group.

"If the Kickapoo Polka Band is connected to them in any way it would be just to fill the empty space left by the disappearance of the barn dances. We lost a lot when those things left us. World War Two was the end of it. The men were all gone. When the war was over the taverns in the towns took over the dances. There was a shift away from the farm.

"I think this is why the music pleases me so. It takes me back to those innocent days. So I like to think wherever the Kickapoo Polka Band is, there would also be a crowd dancing those polkas.

"When a lady called me up to Newry to hear them on Peaceful Valley Road I could swear I could hear dancing feet on a wooden floor along with the music. That was the only time I heard the dancing, I'm sorry to say.

"But I'm confident. I have a good feeling about it. My intuition tells me that when I pass on I'll find that music and these old legs will dance again."

Part Eight

Dane County

Blue Mounds Watcher

THIS COLLECTION HAS many examples of tales that have either their historic or folkloric roots in the Black Hawk War era. We have also seen other examples of "sentinel" ghosts which "guard" specific sites. And many of the stories in this collection bridge eras and cultures.

Blue Mounds has a spirit that captures all of these elements. It also exhibits a peculiar trait of ancient European ghosts.

North American sentinel ghosts—be they American Indian, European-American and even a few African-American—are typically proactive and mobile. Often they are aggressive toward interlopers and wrongdoers.

Europe had an older form of sentinel that is more passive and usually stationary. In the northern part of the European continent and the British Isles there are sentinels known as "watchers." They stand silent guard at castle ruins, abandoned monasteries, mountain passes, and along old Roman roads.

Their origins are ancient. Accounts of their presence go back to the Dark Ages and beyond. They are often thought of as knights bound in the afterlife by pledges to protect made during their earthly quests. They sometimes appear in chain mail and armor, especially in England.

Elsewhere in Europe they appear in robes. Thus the categorization of watchers as ghosts of monks, druids, and mystics of various sorts.

Old European accounts describe watchers as spirits who observe human activity from exposed vantage points. The same ancient source material mentions the frequency of elevated perches such as cathedral spires or castle towers.

The watchers are deemed thoroughly harmless. No account of hostile action toward the living has been recorded.

Perhaps the most unusual aspect of the watchers is their function or purpose. Almost all known ghost types arise out of certain conditions and respond to human activity in somewhat predictable ways. Not so with watchers—they just watch.

The Blue Mounds Watcher does not totally adhere to the European pattern. But it is hard to tell whether the differences are subtle variations or storyteller embellishments.

In this case it was less a matter of a source narrating a tale than of amateur folklorists and historians comparing notes. Please indulge me as I wade into the middle of the story myself.

🔥 🔥 🔥

"So what are you hearing about the excavations of old Fort Blue Mounds?", asked the self-taught archeologist, who was also a graduate student in sociology with eclectic passions for Civil War reenactments and the restoration of timber frame buildings.

His question was directed at three of us at a table at the Hooterville Inn in Blue Mounds. Besides myself there was a high school history teacher and a local businessman.

"They have the old site pretty much outlined," said the businessman. "They have staked out the fortifications and several other buildings. And they've found quite a few artifacts. Everything from kitchen utensils to tools and gun parts."

The conversation took off from there into a review of the various Black Hawk War forts and battle sites. Much of that digression focused on the Department of Natural Resources effort to restore nineteenth-century vegetation at Wisconsin Heights to go with its broader interpretative efforts.

"This is all good stuff for our interests," remarked the teacher. "Even though we might disagree about direction or emphasis, it's a good thing when a government agency or newspaper article brings attention to history, old customs, or even legends. It gets our interests on the agenda, you might say."

Our two other companions were less supportive of this view.

"Don't trust history to the government," grimaced the businessman.

"And the media, they'll take a revered old story and do a tabloid treatment of it," sneered the self-taught archeologist. "Before they're done they throw in the flying saucer treatment and make country people look like fools. Then our ghostbuster friend here comes in after them like the broom crew after the elephant parade and repackages the manure."

When I pressed for a justification for this insult, another half-hour was spent on cheap shots at clearly bogus haunted house stories. Only the teacher rose to my defense.

"Well, we've knocked down all the straw men," stated the educator. "But what about those things *nobody* can explain? And if there's a force or explanation beyond our understanding, what's wrong with calling it a ghost? If we want to pin him down, let's ask him about the Fort Blue Mounds ghost."

And question they did. A straight line through an interrogator's what, when, where, why, and how.

Like preliminary chess moves, my answers only countered and did not defeat their objections. They were realists all, linear in their thought processes, thoroughly secular and devoid of spirituality. Only the educator appreciated the teaching elements of stories. Only the self-taught archeologist showed the slightest facility in the use of imaginative powers. As for the businessman, if a thing could not be added on a ledger, then it did not exist.

The whole exercise reminded me of the large gulf that exists between those who live entirely on the material level and those who are at least partly open to mystery and magic.

At this point, another bar patron inserted himself into our argument and proved to my companions that one could be hard-bitten and yet aware of wonders beyond the recognized senses.

"I couldn't help hearing you talk about the old Blue Mounds ghost," the man with the white beard interjected. "It's always a kick to hear grown men talk in public about things which could get them sent to Mendota. But I've been doing it for years and they haven't caught me yet!"

He was a local handyman. One of those fellows who operates outside of building codes and tax returns. His beat-up pickup sat in front of the Hooterville Inn decorated with a pile of ladders, pipes, boards, and wire spools.

In his late fifties, he was one of those blue-collar guys who hates the aging process yet remains proud of his ability to outwork, outdrink, outfight, and out—(well, we'll leave that aspect unsaid) younger men. The wrinkles on his face said he was as quick to laugh as to fight.

"My family's been seeing that ghost for a hundred and fifty years. The earlier pioneers told my family it was around before that. As to how long, well, there's an argument no one can settle.

"The ghost is a watcher. You probably don't know about that. A watcher stands guard.

"Now some would tell you this is just a ghost who hangs out at one place and plays pocket pool. But there's more to it than that. Watchers have a lot of power over people. They don't have to do anything. They're not in the habit of making people wet their pants. They just get into people's minds.

"I've heard it's like hypnotism. But nothing bad. No kill-your-mother devil messages.

"Mostly it's a calming effect. That's why it's so quiet around here. That ghost takes the lead right out of the pencil of a lot of the troublemakers.

"People use to say it did a better job up at the park than the ranger. That's because it was mostly thought the watcher hung out up on the mound, around the towers and campgrounds.

"As you know from this fort business, it was always more than a campground haunting. Over the years it was seen more by those of us who live here around the fort side. But if you're gonna understand a fort ghost you gotta know how a fort works. You guys look like you're from the draft dodger generation. So I'll explain it to you.

"First there's the fort itself. Probably a blockhouse with stockade and earthworks around it. Then there are pickets or sentries. Sort of your inner perimeter. Then there is an outer perimeter. This outer perimeter with routine scouting and patrolling went as far east as Bohn and Moen Creeks and as far west as Barneveld. And up to Walnut Hollow on Blue Mounds Creek and down to Barber Road.

"How do I know? Well, those are all places where the watcher has been seen. Mostly out on rock bluffs. But sometimes just on the ridge or even up a tree.

"You just need to think about all the places that a lookout could use. The place I've seen him most is down along Ryan and Moyer Roads. But my uncle has seen him plenty along County K in Iowa County north of the park. But he's been seen a few times right outside the bar here. Some say inside, but I've never seen that.

"That brings me to the log tavern part of this. Right where we're sitting there was a log tavern. A place where military leaders, scouts, and such met. No doubt with guards posted outside.

"It fits with what some say about how the watcher got here. Almost always it's a Black Hawk War connection.

"My guess is that the watcher is just a militia lookout who never got called in from his post. But some have more colorful ideas. Everything from the watcher being the guy who was shot in the head at Wisconsin Heights to him being someone brought back from Bad Axe for burial. And buried standing up, they say!

"Others link the watcher to murder victims along the Military Ridge Road. And it's true there was a lot of rough stuff that happened along here in the eighteen twenties and thirties. But almost all of the known crimes were further west. Mostly connected to the old Ridgeway Ghost.

"Then, if you really want to stretch it, there's the older stuff and the voodoo stuff.

"We have that white-haired hippie lady up the back here who claims to be part Indian. Part from Indiana if you ask me.

"She's told me—after three or four Tom and Jerry's—that the watcher was a cursed militia soldier. Somehow the poor bugger tangled with a powerful spirit. Something about a river spirit west of Lone Rock. Some old Indian spirit called a trickster. I couldn't make any sense of it. But I had five or six Tom and Jerry's myself.

"Then there's the even older stuff. Stuff about Blue Mounds being a magical place that has always had a spirit guard. A nun came through the park peddling something to kids about a creation story, the ice age, and the moundbuilders. I'm too Lutheran for that mumbo-jumbo.

"The other thing that gets argued about is the type of ghost. By that I mean his family history. Whether he's Norwegian, German, or Irish. That's a goofy thing to fight about. But they do. They don't know enough history to know that if it is a Black Hawk War militia soldier, then it's ninety-nine percent certain that it was someone from the older eastern states. Not some mackerel-smacker just off the boat. Everybody around here with a grandpop named Ole or Fritz thinks America began when the old boy stepped off the cattle train.

"I half think they picked that up from ghost stories north of Ridge-way. Each group has a Mill Creek story. But those are things you just can't settle. And they shouldn't take away from the fact there is a ghost. I *know*, I've *seen* it.

"You can snicker all you want. And you can bring up a hundred things you can prove didn't happen. That's how it is with ghost stories.

People add on so much in the way of bullmuffins that you lose the basic thing that somebody else saw.

"All I know is that I saw it.

"What it is, well, others can sort that out. I'm comfortable with the guard left out on sentry duty. What he does, well, he watches. It'd be better if more people did that and ran at the mouth less.

"Why, well, I don't have a clue. An old Norwegian who was visiting Little Norway told me a watcher reports to God on human folly. God knows, what with sleeping around, boozing, and carrying on, we got some folly to keep an eye on."

The Voice of Wisconsin Heights

W ISCONSIN HEIGHTS IS forever linked in Wisconsin history to the Black Hawk War. It was the site of the Sac Chief's wily holding action and evacuation.

Within the accounts left behind by territorial militia and U.S. regulars were references to "The Voice." It was said that "The Voice" harangued the troops in a lengthy and emotional speech on the evening before the escape of the Sac.

Various explanation of this event were put forth over the years. The soldiers attributed the speech to Black Hawk himself. Historians suggested the possibility of an impassioned plea to be left alone or a cease-fire request. A few folklorists even alleged an attempted Winnebago intervention.

In northwest Dane County there are those who claim that "The Voice" is not simply an unexplained footnote to a distant event. In the towns of Mazomanie and Roxbury there are sources who insist that "The Voice" persists right down to our day.

"I've heard it and I know others who've heard it," admitted the fisherman and duck hunter. "I spend a fair amount of time out by the river and on the river. I've heard it from the railroad bridge south of Sauk City down to Ferry Bluff.

"You can't understand it. It's not in English. Something in Indian, I would guess. But sometimes you feel in your gut that you know what he's saying. It's something like, 'watch out what you're doing' and 'slow down.' It's a feeling of warning that we don't need to zip around in powerboats and all-terrain vehicles."

🔥 🔥 🔥

"It's a ghost from way back," claimed the Roxbury farmer. "It's from way long before the battle. Probably from back at the time of the mound-builders. I kind of think it is a moundbuilder ghost. You know there are mounds at Wisconsin Heights. As kids we found arrowheads and other things over there. It was more open years ago. The woods are pretty recent.

"You just can't drive up Route 78 and stick your head out the window and hear The Voice. It's got to be a quiet night or dawn. You have to be out of your vehicle and away from the road.

"There are a couple of trails off of Route 78 that will take you up the hill. Some others in off of Taylor Road. But you don't need to go up there to hear. The Voice carries real good. Many hear it in their boats out on the river. I've heard it out by the landing strip on County Y. Some-times I think it's saying something in a sad way. Other times it's more of an angry way."

🔥 🔥 🔥

"It use to scare me as a girl," laughed the grandmother.

"We lived off County Y. Just a little tidy place. I was the oldest of seven girls. So I had morning chores that a boy would ordinarily do. Mine had to do with the chickens.

"I'd heard this grumpy yelling and it felt like someone was watch-ing me. Sometimes I didn't want to leave the house. Mother explained that The Voice was a ghost who couldn't sleep. My, that would make you irritable. And this explanation helped.

"As I grew older I didn't hear it as much. Then I married and moved down to Mazomanie. For years we just drove by. But when my children were grown I had more time to visit and take walks. So I heard it again on an evening walk with my grandson.

"My grandson asked me what it meant. I had never even thought about that part of it. It simply was enough that you could sense the irritation. But my grandson's question started me thinking about it.

"How to go about understanding it was a different matter. Some said it was Sauk Indian language. So it might as well have been Chinese. But later I made friends with a Winnebago lady who played bingo in the Dells. I told her the story and she was interested. She came down one evening to hear for herself.

"My, nothing happened. Good Lord, I was embarrassed. I thought she would think I was crazy. She took it well and said we would try again.

"The second time we heard The Voice. She said she understood little parts of it. The yelling was mostly 'no,' 'get away,' 'stop,' and 'bad.'

"The third time she brought an uncle from Black River Falls. He understood the yelling better. He said it was an old language. It was how Winnebago and Sioux were spoken before the white man came.

"My friend's uncle said The Voice saw everything that went on along his stretch of river. On the evening of our visit, the yelling had to do with someone throwing garbage out of a car, another person throwing bottles in the river, and still another catching fish and killing them and throwing them away.

"The old man explained that this ghost was disturbed by the battle and would not gain peace until the area was again treated as a sacred place.

"How in the world will we get back to that? How do you right all the wrongs of the last one hundred and sixty years?".

Elver's Goblin

WESTERN DANE COUNTY is a gateway of sorts to the rest of southwest Wisconsin. The roads lift into the uplands and the Blue Mounds loom on the western horizon.

But this transition zone is not just a matter of topography. For many generations it has also been a transition zone away from urban influence.

In a variety of folklore collection efforts I have found the area to be the demarcation line for active folklife. West of there you find remnants of old Wisconsin. East of there folklore is mostly a subject of academic interest.

Development pressures virtually guarantee that the cultural base for the oral transmission of folklore—including ghost stories—will soon be a thing of the past. From Mazomanie down to the Green County line the old bachelor farmers and spinsters in the old homesteads are only a few years from displacement by hobby farmers and country estates.

In the meantime we have a few years to visit musty old parlors and write down the old stories.

The Elver's area has generated a number of folktales worthy of interest. Most deal with pioneer life and ethnic groups.

But the Elver's Goblin is a classic American Ghost tale.

A widow in Black Earth enjoys telling the story.

🌿 🌿 🌿

"Every child loves a ghost story," smiled Edith. "There was a time when every child had a favorite local ghost story. Every old house, grave-yard, and dark woods had a story. Our ghosts were as much a part of our community as the priests or the teachers. They were friends even if they were scary.

"I grew up in the Elvers area. Down there we had the Goblin. We were a little proud of him.

"Unlike a lot of ghosts he didn't let us down. By that I mean he appeared regularly. Some ghosts don't do that, you know. They can be fickle. They can be lazy. Or they can fail to show themselves for years.

"Our Goblin was kind enough to appear to anyone foolish enough to seek him out. But that was years ago. I don't know what happens around Elver these days. But in my day we were told many stories and could see for ourselves, too. Or at least hear or otherwise feel the Goblin's presence.

"The Goblin's face was the thing talked about most by those who saw him. He had what you might call a rubbery face. He could twist his face in every way imaginable. He could puff up his head like a balloon. Or he could blow up his chin and throat like a big old bullfrog. Or, my favorite, stick out his tongue about three feet.

"The face showed up in all sorts of strange places. So you had to be on the lookout for him all the time. You might pick up a lid off a pickle crock and see his face in there. Or you might find his head in a laundry basket.

"The men would see that face in grain bins, woodpiles, and in hollow trees. My brother found the laughing head under a stone in the barnyard.

"The Goblin liked to tease the ladies with improper and indecent things. He did things that would get a man arrested these days.

"Quite a few of these outrages happened in outhouses. The men found it funny. They had no idea what a hardship it is for a woman to use an outhouse in the first place. Then to have to worry about a ghost's face coming up through the hole—well that's more than anyone should have put up with!

"But, like I said, it was mostly teasing stuff. No direct injuries were ever talked about. But it was said that a few strangers died of heart attacks brought on by fright.

"My sister had the head come up between her knees when she was taking a bath in a big washtub. Oh, my Lord, the words out of her mouth would have shocked her priest!

"The men had a little story they made up about the Goblin paying special attention to the ladies they called 'old maids.' Old maids to them were any women over thirty who did not swoon over the eligible pool of bald heads and beer bellies.

"But the men had all sorts of barnyard talk about what the Goblin did with those so-called lonely women. I guess it doesn't hurt to have an active imagination—especially if your own life lacks excitement.

"The Goblin took great delight in bothering travelers. Anybody on the road at night could expect a visit. The Goblin could bounce up to them like a ball or crackle up like ball lightning or push up right through the road. He seemed to enjoy doing these things to people from Klevenville, Riley, and Pine Bluff.

"When he appeared in full form he was about five feet tall. But he was barrel-chested with large arms. He had stubby thick legs.

"No one had a real idea of who the Goblin was when he was alive. Oh, there was a little talk about him being a hired man who looked once too often at a farmer's wife. But no one had names or a death to put with that.

"The Goblin dressed like a hired man. But so did everybody around there in those days. Patched pants, soles peeling off his shoes, and frayed collars.

"There was one thing different about him though. A thing where he was ahead of his time. You know how a lot of men today have trouble keeping their trousers up. Back then the men wore suspenders, but the Goblin didn't. His two mounds of rubbery lard peeking out wasn't a pretty sight! Makes one think he was really a plumber!"

Part Nine

Green County

Browntown's Thresher

Farmer ghosts are quite common in New England, New York, and Pennsylvania. There, rustic spirits in Eighteenth century garb still wield sickles in the mists of creek bottom pastures.

One would think that Wisconsin might boast a farmer ghost every quarter section from Hazel Green to Prairie Farm. Oddly enough that is not the case.

Nearly every county in the southern two-thirds of the state has a fragment of a farmer ghost tale. Yet details are sparse and the best information sources have passed away.

My travels through southwest Wisconsin gave me many potential leads on such stories and their locations: Happy Corners, Fayette, Jonesdale, Hazen Corners, Wild Rose, Hill Point, and Liberty. Others may have better luck finding more clues in those places than I did.

The closest I came to the classic colonial-style farm ghost was in southwest Green County. There tempting little bits and pieces about an old time farmer ghost taunted me for three years. Miles of backroad cruising and hours of over-the-fence chat brought me nothing new.

This story, like dozens of others, might have eluded me except for one of those chance encounters that sometimes bless such blind quests.

Fate made me a helper on a friend's run to Illinois to pick up an inheritance of an uncle's sheep flock. That same fate determined that a bald tire on a beat-up livestock trailer would blow out near Martintown.

A man with a walker tottered down to the shoulder of the road to flash a toothless grin at our dilemma. He offered obvious advice as we fumbled with the jack and lug wrench.

The load of sheep served as his invitation to hold forth on old-time farming subjects. One thing lead to another and soon he was talking about Browntown's Thresher.

🌾 🌾 🌾

"All this old-time stuff is quite popular these days. Antique tractors. Reconditioned farm equipment. Draft horses and such. And even groups popping up to hold field days and demonstrations.

"So at first I thought these stories were simply surprise at seeing some old fellow like me show off one of his rigs. But then I remembered there had always been talk of a ghost around Browntown.

"I had a great uncle who lived near the old crossroads of Dill, west of Browntown, who talked about a ghost all the time. That was maybe sixty years ago. And he was talking about things that happened way before that.

"He was a railroad man. He worked the line into Monroe. He said they used to see a ghost along Zander Creek east of Browntown. The ghost would be cutting marsh hay in the meadows along there. He said quite a few people on train crews saw the ghost in those days. Because of location it was easier to see from the tracks than from the road.

"Always the same tall, lean figure in patched, homespun clothing. Always the broad-brimmed hat blocking the face. And always the unusual yellow bandanna loosely tied around the neck.

"The ghost was seen along there for years, I guess. It got so that people only thought it was unusual because the old ghost was cutting hay the old way, by hand with a cradle cutter. But I guess for twenty or thirty years this ghost just went away. Or maybe people just stopped noticing.

"Then maybe twenty years ago we started to hear about a ghost that would be harvesting crops or cutting hay. At first only once or twice a year.

"In the beginning no one put it together with the old ghost. The pattern was a little different. Different places. A little more spread out. But eventually some of us old fellows put it together. It was the time of day and type of place that gave it away.

"It was always in that short time of day when the sun had set but left enough light for another half hour's work. It was always at a place where a woods or a hill on the west put a shadow on the field. Just like what the old railroaders saw along Zander Creek.

"Well, as time went on this whole thing got so a few of us understood how the old ghost and the more recent stuff fit together. We patched together the stories. Collected them, you might say.

"Most people didn't really know what they saw. We might be at the drafthorse field day over by Darlington and someone would ask if we knew the old fellow with the blue roan team. Or down at the Monroe tractor pull someone might ask about the man with the steam tractor.

"That's how it went. A little question here. A little third-hand story there. It really showed more things than I ever expected. Changes and differences I mean. Almost like a history lesson in farming.

"Sometimes it's horsepower. Usually the blue roan team. Once in awhile with some big standardbreds.

"When it's horsepower it will usually be hay-related. Mostly mowing with a simple five-foot International sickle mower. But sometimes loading loose hay with a loader. Funny, though, no one sees any raking.

"Sometimes it's steampower. The big old son-of-a-bucks with the thirty-foot drive belts. Then it's usually threshing or chopping. This steam tractor usually stands out in people's minds. Not just for size, but because of that whistle. Like the whistles you used to hear on tugboats or at a foundry around shift change.

"Then sometimes it's antique gas tractors. Mostly John Deeres pulling grain binds or corn binds. But sometimes threshing or mowing, too.

"Threshing is the most common thing. Or at least having the machine up and running. Cause sometimes no one's feeding bundles. But anyhow, that's how the old fellow picked up the name of the Brown-town Thresher.

"But, truth be known, he's seen doing all sorts of work. Shocking corn, stacking sheaves, running a buzz saw, or even using old threshing flails and winnowing baskets.

"The real arguments come over whether he's always alone. If you know anything you know that a lot of these things are not one man jobs. Yet, no one is completely sure of any helpers.

"One report talked about a crew. But the time and place just didn't fit. So we kind of wrote that one off.

"There's kind of a side story too. The Browntown Thresher has a helper side to him. This is sort of like all the old chore helper ghosts we've always had in the country.

"You know, the ones who split your wood or fix your fence.

"But one of these times I'm going to turn the table on him. I'm going to catch him on that grain bind and get up in that rear seat and lay those bundles down in a straight line just like my Grandpop taught me."

Green County's Käsegeist

Eᴛʜɴɪᴄ ɢʜᴏsᴛs ᴀʀᴇ not in short supply in Wisconsin. As this collection shows, there are few ghost stories that lack a reference to the origins or group identifications of the principals in the tale.

Germanic ghosts are especially abundant in Wisconsin. Although they reach their highest numbers in areas outside the reach of this collection (southeast Wisconsin, the Lake Michigan cities up to Two Rivers, and a Wausau to Eau Claire belt), they are found in each southwest county.

These Germanic ghosts are not always German in a national origin sense. Because many of the immigrants from the growing German state were freethinkers and political progressives they were not often attuned to the storytelling tradition of their peasant past.

Germanic ghost traditions in Wisconsin tend to owe their continuation to the German-speaking immigrants from Austria, southeast France, northwest Bohemia, Poland, and Switzerland.

It will come as no surprise that Green County leads the way with Swiss stories. Monroe and New Glarus offer many tales of ghostly alpenhorns and yodelling.

In addition there are hints of Swiss pioneer ghosts throughout the western half of Green County. Among them: A Zentner Road Milk Maid, a Burgy Creek Horseman, a Skinner Hollow Woodchopper, and a party of Cadiz Springs Yeagers (hunters). But like most of the hundreds of references to local spirits in southwest Wisconsin the Swiss ghosts of Green County are mainly fragments of older tales.

One Swiss tale retains much of the flavor and enough of the details to make it a unique Wisconsin ghost story: The Green County Käsegeist. A Käsegeist is a cheese ghost. What more appropriate spirit for the land of the cheeseheads?

A retired Monticello cheesemaker tells the tale with warmth and ownership. The story is part of a broad repertoire of cheesemaking and cheese factory folklore.

"This is more than a cheese factory ghost," warned Rollie. "We have cheese factory ghosts all over Wisconsin, so that's not what makes this special. It is more like a spirit of the cheese itself. You know, almost like a ghost and patron saint put together.

"This is not an easy story to tell. I've heard it told many different ways and about many different places.

"Years ago this was a New Glarus story. That was in my grandfather's day, back when lots of the old Swiss were around. I'm only quarter Swiss through Granddad. But I was raised in the Swiss Church so I have a feel for the old Switzers.

"The old Switzers told this story at many places, everywhere they went to make cheese. There was a Belleville version where the ghost lived in an old warehouse. In the Juda version the ghost was always associated with the old-style milk cans. Browntown's story revolved around cheese shipments on the old Milwaukee Road. I've heard some odd things about the ghost at the Town Hall co-op in the Town of Washington. Same deal over in Argyle in Lafayette County.

"It wasn't just the location and circumstances that varied. It was the way the ghost showed himself, too.

"You could call this an Old World ghost because it didn't have the simple haunting habits of American ghosts. Sometimes it appeared as a man in traditional Swiss costume who would visit taverns and buy rounds. Other times it appeared as a hovering light over the vats and tanks.

"There's something else to this Käsegeist. Something about the essence of cheese. Especially about the old recipes for the special cheeses.

"There's magic and secrets in cheesemaking. The master cheesemakers had the knowledge. They brought something extra to the process. And some say this extra was something inspired by the ghost, or maybe was the ghost himself.

"Ask the master brewers or the master bakers. There is always something else that goes into good beer or good bread. It's the same with cheese.

"The story I know best comes out of this tradition of the magic of cheesemaking. It's the story of the ghost at Poplar Grove.

"Now there's argument over whether there is a place called Poplar Grove. There is a Poplar Grove Road off of Highway 39 west of New Glarus. And there is disagreement over whether there was a cheese factory there and how long ago. Or whether an old Switzer cheesemaker lived out there.

"Some place this so-called Poplar Grove cheese factory on Buckeye Road. Some say it really was at the old settlement of Postville. Both are in the Town of York, along with Poplar Grove Road. So it's somewhere over there in the northwest corner of the county. My money is at the Poplar Grove Road location right near the Erickson farm on Highway 39.

"But none of the location squabble is as interesting as the claims made about this ghost.

"The old Switzer master cheesemaker—different old people called the Swiss by the names switzers, sweitzers, or schweissen—was known to have a special recipe or formula for making the best cheese around. This was long ago. A hundred years or more. Back before cheese became a big business in Wisconsin.

"Most people don't realize that the cheese business built up real slow. You have to remember that the state was settled by self-reliant home-steaders. Sales of farm products were limited to a few hogs or maybe a wagon or two of grain. That didn't really change until the railroads reached all the small towns. Suddenly, then, you could reach those city markets.

"The old Switzer out at Poplar Grove had been making cheese all along. But just for sale in New Glarus, Blanchardville, and Hollandale. The story goes that he got drunk in New Glarus one night on his cheese sale money. On the way home his horse threw him. Then the ghost walked him home and told him how to expand the cheese business.

"The ghost correctly pointed out that Wisconsin is more suited to grazing than to grain production. And the ghost pointed out—again correctly in those times—that raw milk was bulky and spoiled quickly.

"The upshot of the ghost's walking lecture was the vision of a Wisconsin with a cheese factory in every town, spaced so that farmers could haul milk there in between morning and evening milking. And the ghost told the old Switzer that the two of them would help realize this dream.

"That's how it all began. The old Switzer and the ghost traveled around planting the idea and helping people get set up. It's also part of the story that the ghost contributed something of his special essence to these new cheese factories. This gave Wisconsin an edge in quality cheese.

"That brings us to the next part of the story. You know you can't have anything good without someone else wanting it. So the old Switzer had to put up with break-ins where robbers searched for a book of secret knowledge. Many were frightened off by the ghost.

"Eventually a group of businessmen from Illinois hired some professional gangsters to steal the information. Or beat it out of the old Switzer.

"The bullies came by train to New Glarus. They stayed at a hotel there. They rented horses and one evening went out to take care of the old Switzer.

"No one knows for sure what happened out at Poplar Grove. The old Switzer said he heard the door downstairs being kicked in, then heard five or six men screaming, then quiet.

"The criminals were found in the following days roaming naked in the fields. Supposedly their eyes were bugged out, they were drooling, and they couldn't talk.

"A local constable put them back on the train to Illinois. They sat still as statues. That is, until somebody offered them some good New Glarus cheese. Then they went stark raving nuts and had to be tied and put in the baggage car.

"That's about all I know concerning the Käsegeist. Except for his connection to limburger production. But that's not really a Green County story."

Boner's Ghost

THE STORY OF Boner's Ghost is not only the last story in this collection, it is also the last story to be completed in terms of both writing and traveling.

Boner's Ghost first came to my attention in the late nineteen-eighties. The story was making the rounds of frontier re-enactment camps and was told around campfires with a half-dozen other tales of pioneer ghosts.

The story was a little short on historical details. It was simply said that Boner was Wisconsin's first European-American murder victim. The color in the story was left to the terror evoked by the screaming and crying ghost.

Oddly enough Boner's Ghost popped up in connection to the Ridgeway Ghost, Helena's Rowdy Ghosts, and with many Wisconsin River valley ghosts from Sauk City to Prairie du Chien. The connection was never firm enough to merit inclusion in those stories, however. It was as if the sources simply threw in Boner's Ghost for good measure. Like dozens of other ghost stories, it might have stayed on my second string for further exploration at a future date.

This time it was no series of odd coincidences or quirky chance encounters that resuscitated the story. Instead, it was real historical research that fleshed out the tale and spurred me on.

A swiftly approaching deadline for a promised article on early southwest Wisconsin breweries for the Iowa County Historical Society newsletter sent me scurrying to libraries. On level ten at the State Historical Society library I scooped up the Green County collection and lugged it to one of those little tables at the end of the stacks.

Few of the Green County books shed any light on my research topic. My last hope resided in the *History of Green County - 1884*, one of those combined efforts of boosterism and local history preservation that swept Wisconsin in the late nineteenth century.

While scanning the pioneer section my eyes were drawn to the names Boner and McNutt. The paragraphs that followed confirmed that this was the Boner of Boner's Ghost and also fleshed out the circumstances of his demise. The grisly foundation for at least one ghost story, and perhaps two or more, was there in the "official record."

Boner and McNutt are acknowledged in that volume as Green County's first permanent European-American residents. They settled at the "Sugar River Diggings" in 1827. The location was somewhat vague but was said to be in the present day Town of Exeter. The account refers to the northeast quarter of Section 34.

The two pioneers built a log trading post and commenced trade with local Indians for furs and lead. They soon sought the services of a translator to expand their trade with the local tribes. The position went to Van Sickle, who had experience throughout the old Northwest Territory. Van Sickle spoke Sac, Winnebago, and Potowatomi.

The operation thrived.

What happened next is not clear. There is no chronicle of conflict between the three men or of disputes with local tribes. What is known is that McNutt became Wisconsin's first recorded European-American winter madness case. This severe case of cabin fever brought McNutt to the point where he hacked up Boner with an axe after a prolonged drinking bout.

It is thought this happened in early 1828, probably no later than February of that year. It is unclear where Van Sickle was during the incident. One can speculate that he prudently hid under a pile of hides.

However, Van Sickle soon fled to the fort at Blue Mounds. McNutt followed, though it is unclear whether he was in pursuit with witness eradication in mind or simply heading for the nearest inhabited site.

In any event McNutt surrendered to authorities and confessed. Van Sickle corroborated the story.

McNutt was taken to Prairie du Chien, then the seat of government, for incarceration and trial. The civilian jail was deemed insufficient and so McNutt was entrusted to the military at Fort Crawford.

The records are vague after that point. It seems that there was a trial in July of 1828. But the sentence given to the defendant was not mentioned in the accounts. Presumably McNutt was found guilty based on his confession. But folklore suggests a variety of dispositions. Some say he died in custody. Others talk of a long term served and an eventual move to Iowa. A Prairie du Chien legend tells of a hanging. In some accounts he was paroled during the Black Hawk War and gleefully redeemed himself in blood at Bad Axe. In other accounts he was killed during that conflict.

It is fitting that Boner's Ghost serves as the last chapter in this collection. The story brings me full circle in my search for themes that run through southwest Wisconsin ghost stories.

I do not wish to overstate the connections between distinct ghost tales. Clearly there are heirloom and whimsical stories as idiosyncratic as their sources. But my gut tells me there are some common threads that run through many southwest Wisconsin stories.

The "pieces" of the Boner's Ghost "puzzle" further convince me of these connections.

Join me as I revisit some of my sources for earlier stories and wonder, as I do , if they knew of these connections all along.

"Sure, I heard of that Boner's Ghost," said the Vernon County treasure-seeker.

"You never asked me about that. All the oldtimers knew about Boner's Ghost. Shoot, it was Wisconsin's first ghost story.

"I didn't tell you before, but some used to say that the ghost up on Wildcat Mountain was a McNutt. I never believed it.

"And it sure wasn't the old murderer McNutt. The events are over fifty years apart. But was a younger McNutt involved in the Billings gang? I can't really say.

"I kinda think it was just something that people plugged in. You know, just like how they use Benedict Arnold's name for traitors. McNutt just got plugged in wherever something crazy was going on."

"So you're still chasing that Boner's Ghost business?" queried the pretend Scottish storyteller from the Bloody Lake Rendezvous.

"Boner's Ghost is well known in rendezvous and reenactment circles. He's sort of the patron saint of winter madness in the Midwest.

"The interplay between Boner, McNutt, and Van Sickle—three crazy white guys if there ever were any—and the Indians is also legendary. I think you could say that their escapades provide the framework for many Indian and white interaction stories.

"There's a farm three miles east of New Glarus where there are screams at night that are said to be Boner's Ghost.

"Even the other two remain a fixture in local lore. Van Sickle is a name given to a ghost arising from the Spafford Creek Massacre. McNutt is connected by name to the fight to the death at the Battle of the Pecatonica.

"Were Van Sickle or McNutt tied in to the Hermit stories?" asked one of my Mill Creek sources rhetorically. "I wouldn't think so. The ethnic groups and timelines are a little off. Only Van Sickle sounds anything like the Mill Creek Hermit. But some of the story elements could have rubbed off and stuck to local stories. I could see how that could easily happen.

"I have a brother-in-law down in Monroe who told me two things about the Boner's Ghost story. One was about how the McNutt family in Green County changed their names to McNitt. He said that a McNitt paid off the family blood debt while serving in the Thirteenth Wisconsin Regiment in the Civil War. Apparently he saved a lot of Green County boys in the Tennessee engagements.

"Another was that Boner, McNutt, and Van Sickle function as a ghost trio. Yeah. He said the Monroe story is that Boner now chases McNutt with the axe and that Van Sickle tries to intervene. Supposedly this mad chase goes on along Highway 39 between New Glarus and Hollandale and up Highway K to Barneveld.

"He mentioned something about galloping horses. But you know, I think that's really from other Hollandale ghosts."

❧ ❧ ❧

"Remember, I told you it was all in good fun," came the reminder from the Avoca descendant of the Morrey Creek Medicine Woman.

"Now, I'm not so sure. I thought we had learned that Winny Beaujeau was a trickster spirit with Indian roots. Just a cut-up or comedian. But your questions got me looking into it deeper. I really wanted to understand it. That's when I happened upon the Boner's Ghost story.

"I think there's a link to the wintertime craziness we have in Wisconsin. I found that Winny Beaujeau had a bigger range than I thought. Really the whole length of the Wisconsin River and its tributaries. It's really a creature of the river.

"If you look into it, you'll find that there were quite a few bloody trading post murders. Many share a common theme of a visit from an one-eyed Indian medicine man. Usually the medicine man asks to have something without paying. When he's rejected there's a curse put on the trading post. You can guess the rest.

"My hunch is that Boner and McNutt were paid a visit by our trickster.

"Now, the next thing will seem strange. The old guy with the glass eye over in Gotham claims to be a Boner descendant. Of course he claims to be descended from Governor Dodge and some Winnebago prophet, too.

"The old guy says that Boner's Ghost is still wandering. Says he saw it along Military Ridge at spots from Ridgeway to Preston. Says that Boner had his eyes gouged out and is searching for where McNutt tossed them.

ǖ ǖ ǖ

We often assume that we have all of the time in the world to renew acquaintances and catch up on shared interests. But the ticking clock of mortality just as often proves us wrong.

So I was reminded when I read the obituary of the retired teacher who lived near Clyde. There would be no more background on Wisconsin River stories from that source. No more warm greetings or heartfelt encouragement for this collection of tales. His warnings still stick in my mind, as did his advice to remain open to possibilities. I felt severely cheated by the removal of the opportunity to share the stories with him.

A visit with his family helped me close the chapter on our friendship and on this book. His eldest daughter brought two cups of cider to a comfortable book-lined nook in his cottage. We exchanged the usual pleasantries and memories. Then she lowered her voice to a whisper so that other mourners would not hear her.

"I know Dad shared some unusual things with you," she said tentatively. "Many people thought dad a little strange or eccentric. Almost like a latter day C.S. Lewis. But I know he was deeply passionate about his interests and his beliefs. I flatter myself that I was the only one in the family who listened to him.

"He kept track of you. He was quite fond of you. You could go where he no longer had energy to go. He followed your folklore books and your historical society articles. He said he could chart you on a map from that evidence and could guess what other stories you have discovered but had not written about yet. He should have been a detective.

"He was interested in Boner's Ghost too. He even had me drive him to Monroe to do some research. But his interest was not in Boner. He was pursing a theory about a connection between horrible crimes in Wisconsin. He thought that McNutt was possessed by an evil force. That force continues on to today.

"You know we have some strange things happening in our part of the world. Horrible murders and disappearances that are out of character for our peaceful rural areas. Dad thought that the McNutt incident held the key to understanding this evil force. Although it was more complicated than that. Something about the Sinsinawa, Belmont, and Platteville Mounds. Tied in with a sentinel spirit at Blue Mounds and Effigy Mounds along the Wisconsin River.

"A lot of that went over my head. He would get so agitated when he was talking about it that it scared me. But I know there's one part he wanted me to pass on. The part on the American Indian connection.

"Dad finally came to the conclusion that this evil force lived off a certain turmoil in the spirit world. The turmoil in turn he attributed to the unresolved tension between the spirits attached to the American Indians and those attached to the European-Americans. And he felt that there were cross-bred spirits that were the most conflicted of all.

"He felt that we are all linked together, whether we like it or not. He saw a need to work on a 'medicine of peace.' He thought the best place for you to start would be with Boner's Ghost.

"He wanted you to put it to rest."